GODBODYISM

How Adamology Leads to a True Black Thearchy

BLACK DIVINITY SERIES VOL 5

SHAHIDI ISLAM

This publication has been made to provide accurate and authoritative information with regard to the subject matter discussed. It is sold with the understanding that neither the publisher nor the author are engaging in the offering of medical, psychological, or sociological service. If any of the above are required a competent professional person should be consulted.

All quotations provided throughout this book are strictly for the purpose of education and research and fall well into the guidelines of fair dealing. Fair dealing is recognised in Canada, the United Kingdom, and Australia and allows for individuals, researchers, musicians, educators, and authors to use copyrighted material without permission from the copyright owner.

Book Ordering Information
Email: enquiries@divineblackpeople.com
https://divineblackpeople.com
Printed in the United States of America

Attention African American Theologians!!!

Learn Now a Black Cosmology Designed Purely for the Ghetto

The Universal Order of Things is the fifth instalment in Shahidi Islam's *Black Divinity Series.* Is there an ideal cosmology for Black people? How about for Black ghetto people? Shahidi Islam provides a type of the cosmology he learned growing up in Brooklyn, New York. To learn more about it shop now.

The Universal Order of Things

This book is dedicated to the Gods and
Goddesses of the foundation,
who dwell in a Nation of love, peace, and
happiness

Table of Contents

Series Preface

The current *Black Divinity Series* was originally written to create a new kind of Black theology: a Black Godbody Theology. The starting point for this theology is that all Black people are divine, yet this concept of Black divinity actually has a long history. It was first articulated by the ancient Ethiopians over twenty-eight millennia ago, in a land that was called in times past Ta Neteru (the land of the gods and goddesses). The message was then continued on in ancient Egypt by the various mystical traditions, around another nine millennia ago; and by the ancient Hebrew mystical traditions over three millennia ago. The message was eventually lost to the Hebrews during their many exiles, but it was still maintained in ancient Egypt and ancient Ethiopia over the vast centuries.

Then came the Baptist to revive among the Judeans the understanding of Black divinity. He would also start a liberation movement among the Judeans, predicting the coming of someone after him, in his own lifetime, who would bring the people back to their Black divinity through a baptism into holiness and into a fully independent monarchy. The very Messiah he prophesied, would continue on that message, which after his disappearance splintered off into several separate branches.

The mystics among his followers were called the gnostics and they combined the Messiah's message with the ancient Egyptian philosophy. The gnostic message thereby continued the idea of Black divinity secretly and underground during a time when even the mainstream messianic movement was also underground (due mainly to heavy persecution). Unfortunately, when the messianic movement, finally, did gain legality it was only the mainstream version. Gnosticism, however, would remain an outlaw movement, thus driving them even further underground.

At that time, within the mainstream movement the only Black person considered truly divine was the Messiah (back then the only images of the Messiah were as a Black man). Black divinity then re-emerged with Islamic mysticism, a tradition that combined the gnostic oral tradition with Islamic interpretations of the Quran. The Prophet himself was an ardent follower of gnostic ideas and beliefs. It is even likely that he was trained and mentored by a practicing gnostic. Whether this is true or not, we know for sure that he referenced several gnostic teachings and traditions in the Quran that he could not have possibly known without having some familiarity with their history.

Finally, Black divinity would ultimately reach its greatest height in America, starting with the Honorable Elijah Muhammad bringing to the Black communities of America that Islamic mystical tradition through his Lost-Found Nation of Islam. From the Nation of Islam would then eventually emerge the godbody movement: a movement in the ghetto that went on to define G.O.D. as guns over drugs—thereby interpreting that the militant Black man that gains Knowledge 120 becomes a God in his own right, having the power to give life (through spreading 120) and to take life (we all know how); and to build; and to destroy.

Now for the most part we try to use this power, not to take life, but to build through it a Nation of Gods and Earths (hereafter to be called Goddesses).

That said, the 120 lessons we godbodies endorse are, again, only just the Supreme Wisdom lessons of the Honorable Elijah Muhammad. In that sense they have been read and mastered by several heroes and heroines within the Black community including: Minister Louis Farrakhan, Minister Malcolm X, Imam Warith Deen Muhammad, Dr. Khalid Muhammad, Dr. Sebi Alfredo Bowman, Dr. Malachi Z. York, the Champ Muhammad Ali, Erikah Badu, Bilal the 1st Born, D'Angelo, Jay Electronica, Busta Rhymes, Rakim Allah, Nas, Foxy Brown, Queen Latifah, all of the Fugees, the Wu-Tang Clan, Mobb Deep, and Brand Nubian. Even so, while the United States government has attacked and attempted to discredit many of these Black leaders, all of them are still well beloved by most Black people. The truth is, we Black people have always had the potential for divinity, but it is only now that we are starting to realise how to actually achieve it.

True, it may be currently accepted among the godbody – again, the ghetto organisation that is currently the central body propagating the message of Black divinity – that once a city, a nation, and the world comes to accept the truth of our destiny then a Black thearchy will begin to exist upon the earth. Indeed, as any true solarpunk/ecofuturist would much rather aim and strive for a low-tech and high-empath future; even so, within the godbody a more ghetto combination of solarpunk and Neo-Soul is believed to be more desirable; but that mainly through Black people taking their place as a God-Collective of the divine Black people we have always been.

Series Introduction

The current series is based on notes originally written in 2006 and edited in 2012 and again in 2022 for the purpose of liberating my people. Contained within are also a very large cross-section of quotations that break up a lot of the content making it seem at times frustrating and a little hard to read. This annoyance was unavoidable due to the current situation, and the unfortunate mistrust of those outside of the street life of the intelligence of anyone arising out of the street life. Again, hopefully no one within the street life, particularly within the Five Percent Nation, will be too offended by some of the language that I have chosen to use throughout, as it was mainly for the purpose of speaking to the uninitiated, not to ruin our image or desecrate our culture.

From an historical context all past developments in human progress have been correlated to philosophical precursors. From Aristotle's influence on ancient Greece and Plato's influence over the Roman *res publica*; to the influence of Rousseau on the French Revolution and Marx on the Russian; it is virtually impossible to separate historical epochs from their philosophical precursors. The initial philosophical bursts of light and hope, however, usually begin to dim as the pains of reaction begin to set in. This reactionary response to the new ideas and the hostility of its opposition usually bring great sorrow and disillusionment to the representatives of the new vision and ideal.

As these realities are the historical norm for all prior to revolutionary changes it is clear that anything of this calibre will meet also its own huge bursts of reactionary opposition and rage. From church pulpit to political gathering, from social clubs to cultural events all groups and sections of society claim allegiance to morality and against the dark cloud of the street life. True indeed, as the streets are considered a curse on society, and themselves cursed of God, we, in the eyes of those outside of the streets, should have nothing to do with anything even resembling the theocentric, let alone the thearchic. In fact, our anti-establishment makes us seem to any who are not affiliated to be more nihilistic than ritualistic. This anti-establishment being a product of our rejection by the establishment and being outcasts to it, has caused us to question our place in a society that would create and tolerate such vicious injustices as occur in the neighbourhoods of this so-called Western society.

But the Black thearchy itself is really just a system based on the identification of a new Black theodicy, that is, a study of God's goodness and righteousness from a Black person's perspective. Having arisen from the backstreets of New York as the godbody, we have taken their general outlook and message, and added to them theological, psychological, ideological, sociological, ecological, and cosmological depth. Conversely, though, the Black thearchy is primarily based on the use of godbody codes and culture to achieve Black identity amid the difficult and adverse situations of racism, poverty, humiliation, demonisation, dyseducation, discrimination, marginalisation, criminalisation, and state-orchestrated incarceration.

As a people most of we Blacks have been separated from our history and a knowledge of our history; but as Nature expresses herself through a cyclical rhythm of spontaneous repetitions, I feel that a knowledge of recent Black history is worth acknowledging. Marcus Garvey inspired an entire generation with the thought of a Black God. A God, not White like their slave-masters (or like their job-managers in this current system of wage-slavery) but a God Black like them, who understood the trials and sufferings of the people and offered them the strength and power to redeem themselves from these sufferings.

This philosophy spread in Africa, America, and the Caribbean in many forms. Two most obvious forms were the Rastafarians, who claimed Negusa Negast Tafari was the Black God incarnate, and the Black theologians, who claimed the Messiah Jesus was the Black God incarnate. But you also had the Black Muslims, who claimed Master Fard Muhammad was the Black God incarnate. Then you had the Afrocentrics who claimed the ancestral gods of Africa (particularly those of ancient Egypt), which manifest themselves in Nature, were the Black gods incarnate. Even the Kemetic scholars (who are commonly and derisively called "Hoteps" by most Black people) would claim the Egyptian god Ra to be the Black God incarnated in all Black males; similar to the Five Percent, who claim Allah to be *the God* incarnated in all Black males who have mastered the 120 lessons and opened the third eye of astral vision.

All that said, the basis for the current *Black Divinity Series* is six categorical systems which are instituted within the godbody movement to allow for our further continuance: Black divinity, Black revolutionism, Black eroticism, Black astralism, Black demodernisation, and Black syndicalism. These all effectively spell up to the words: Black DREADS; and all also make up the godbody ideology that I endorse –

and are generally accepted within the godbody movement as a whole – though they have never been spelled-out or outlined in this sort of way before. What I thereby hope to accomplish with this undertaking is a complete renewal of our movement and the lessons of the movement as handed down to me by my mentor and enlightener so as to show where our movement can lead and why the actual teleology of godbodyism will be a positive and not a self-destructive one.

In itself the godbody theory articulated throughout has been designed to be a form of Black ideology that incorporates ideas, language, and expressions from chaos theory, deconstruction theory, decolonising theory, post-colonial theory, critical race theory, pro-Black anarchist theory, and pro-sex womanist theory into the outlook and world vision of the Five Percent Nation. And as stated earlier the Five Percent Nation as a movement teaches that the Black man is God. Beginning in the 1960s under the leadership of a direct disciple of Malcolm X, who at that time was named Clarence 13X, but who we call Allah out of respect for the vision he received of the potential divinity of all Black men, obviously including himself, we seek also to enlighten our people as to their potential.

The traditions of the godbody movement founded by Allah are, again, based on the 120 lessons, which in themselves are really just the Supreme Wisdom lessons of the Honorable Elijah Muhammad. In that sense they have been read and mastered by several heroes and heroines within the Black community: Minister Louis Farrakhan, Minister Malcolm X, Imam Warith Deen Muhammad, Dr. Khalid Muhammad, Dr. Sebi Alfredo Bowman, Dr. Malachi Z. York, Muhammad Ali, Jay Electronica, Busta Rhymes, Erikah Badu, Ice Cube, Rakim Allah, Nas, Mobb Deep, the Wu-Tang Clan, and Brand Nubian. Furthermore, while the

United States government has attacked and attempted to discredit many of these Black leaders here mentioned, all of them are still well beloved by the Black community in general.

Nevertheless, my central cause for rewriting *Black Divinity* as a series was not just so as to create a new ideology and sociology for Black people, but more so to make a kind of ghetto theology, a Black Godbody Theology, for our overall empowerment. It cannot be denied that the godbody has a theology as we all share a general theory of God, of the devil, and of righteousness. Yet, as an African American theology the godbody theology can still be differentiated from that of the classical model of African American theology. If we take as an example the four degrees of faith (Skousen 2017): from no faith, to little faith, to great faith, to complete faith, we can see that classical African American theology features most of these four levels: the humanists have no faith, the liberationists/womanists have great faith, and the prosperous have complete faith. Well, we godbodies complete the cipher by having little faith, believing God to exist mainly in natural phenomena like a Universal Intelligence, the Universal Laws, the Original Black man, and all Original people.

Basically, it is the aim and purpose of this book to represent the godbody movement by, firstly, seeking to introduce the godbody theology as an African American theology nuanced from Cone's in that it is not a survival theology but a thrival theology; a thrival theology that came out of the ghetto experience to give to the Black people of the ghetto the hope for a better future, one which they themselves create. Herein, Black Godbody Theology is a ghetto theology that promotes Black improvement and empowerment; even as James Cone himself stated, "Unless theology can become 'ghetto theology,' a theology that speaks to black people, the gospel message has no promise of life for the black man – it is a lifeless message" (Cone 2021: 37).

Even so, it must obviously also be noted that a lot of the ideas and practices encouraged throughout are not those of the entire godbody of the United States, but are add-ons I developed based on lessons I learned in the Socialist Workers Party as an anti-capitalist and in the Black Church as a Pentecostal. As I left America as a "newborn" godbody I never had the chance to fully master the 120 lessons; I did, however, take a lot of the lessons I learned in cipher with the godbody and expound on them to co-create with my enlightener: God Born Supreme Allah, a Black thearchy based on his own GBSA-ideology. This book therefore is mainly a union of all the previous movements I learned from so as to contribute to the further empowering of our people.

Recognising also that a lot of the Gods themselves have no tolerance for innovation; I concluded that we stand no hope of ever overthrowing White supremacy without making certain changes to our lessons. We will never elevate until we are willing to innovate. And if we were to find that something was emphatically wrong we would be obliged to destroy it and so elevate beyond it, even as we destroy the mathematics of anyone who does not backup their lessons with proof. It is my hope that these lessons, which are mainly based on quotations, can be used by all other newborns to understand how the Gods build, and by godbodies to bring us to a place of true divinity in our ways and actions based on knowledge, wisdom, and under-standing. True indeed, as the highest form of understanding is love, even so, the highest form of love is libidinal, it is by this kind of love that we will be able to elevate beyond local hood heroes to become global superheroes.

Finally, it is my intention for the current approach to be used to inform the course of the godbody movement in its rise to popularity, and to create an avenue for the acceptance of this theological perspective within the current discussions of African American theology. Within this context I pay homage to those who came before me in the classical schools: Anthony B. Pinn, William R. Jones, James H. Cone, Albert B. Cleage, Delores S. Williams, Kelly B. Douglas, Robert S. Beckford, Anthony G. Reddie, Creflo A. Dollar, and Thomas D. Jakes. Still, it must also be said at this point that although I am myself a fellow of the Society for the Study of Theology, all the ideas and outlooks presented in this book are overwhelmingly my own and nobody else's. Peace.

The Supreme Mathematics

Potentials

k = knowledge (1)

w = wisdom (2)

u = understanding (3)

f = freedom – I choose not to add culture as freedom is the most obvious elevation from understanding and culture is implied in the whole mathematics (4)

p = power – (I use the term power neither in the Marxian sense, as in to dominate nor in the Foucauldian sense, as in to discipline or surveille; but instead use it in the Adlerian sense as in empowerment) I choose not to add refinement as power is the next elevation from freedom and progresses till it reaches equality (5)

e = equality (6)

G – God   where God is equivalent to the omnipresent, and not to a state of pure perfection (7)

B = build – when adding on (8)

D = destroy – when subtracting (8)

$\forall$ = born (9)

$\circ$ = cipher (0)

Symbols

D = dialectical moment where *pa* > *na* becomes *na* > *pa*, or vice versa.

Lm = the limitation

∃ = when there is

+ = together with

∈ = the sum includes

> = greater than

≥ = greater than or equal to

< = lesser then

≤ = lesser than or equal to

→ = leads on to

↔ = if and only if

↗ = on the increase

↘ = on the decrease

∝ = proportional to

Values

∞ = infinity

o = zero

λ = wavelength

A = amplitude

d = displacement

t = time expended

v = rate of velocity

δ = astral forces $-> x^1$

α = social forces $-> x^{10}$

β = global forces $-> x^{20}$

θ = environmental forces $-> x^{30}$

ϕ = terrestrial forces (also called geomagnetic forces) $-> x^{40}$

ϑ – solar forces (also called heliospheric magnetic forces) – $> x^{50}$

∂ = globular forces (also called stellar magnetic forces) $-> x^{60}$

φ = galactic forces (also called galactic magnetic forces) $-> x^{70}$

ψ = super-clusteral forces (also called intercluster magnetic forces) $-> x^{80}$

ε = cosmic forces $- > x^{90}$

Pa = positive action of an individual

pa = positive action of a social body

Na = negative action of an individual

na = negative action of a social body

x = social potential of a social body

n = level of social potentiality

g = a social movement

$opp.\,g$ = an oppressing social movement

$emp.\,g$ = an empowering social movement

(pa) = all the positive actions of a social body

(na) = all the negative actions of a social body

(v) = all the social velocity

(g) = the whole social movement

S = decelerative force caused by reaction of social body x_1

R = accelerative force caused by resistance of social body x_2

S = syndicalism

The Godbody System

The Universal Laws of Existence

1. The law of interaction (whose corollary is the pleasure principle),

2. The law of intersubjectivity (whose corollary is the vibratory law),

3. The law of self-organisation (whose corollary is the identity law),

4. The law of opposition (whose corollary is the polarity law),

5. The law of repetition (whose corollary is the inertia law),

6. The law of self-similarity (whose corollary is the correspondence law),

7. The law of conservation (whose corollary is the reciprocity law),

8. The law of evolution (whose corollary is the power law),

9. The law of devolution (whose corollary is the entropy law),

10. The law of self-destruction (whose corollary is the phase-transition law),

11. The law of interconnectivity (whose corollary is the synchronicity law), and

12. The law of interrelation (whose corollary is the eternalist law).

The 10 Principles

1. No God but Allah

2. No power imbalances

3. No non-authors

4. No non-fighters

5. No Divine fights alone

6. No problems handled in the Square should ever leave the Square

7. No marriage or marriages

8. No missing parliament meetings

9. No underwear ever

10. No harassment or rape of any kind ever

What We Teach

1. That Black people are the Original people of the planet earth.

2. That Black people are the fathers and mothers of civilization.

3. That the science of Supreme Mathematics is the key to understanding man's relationship to the universe.

4. That Islam is a natural way of life, not a religion.

5. That education should be fashioned to enable us to be self sufficient as a people.

6. That each one should teach one according to their knowledge.

7. That the Black man is god and his proper name is ALLAH. Arm, Leg, Leg, Arm, Head.

8. That our children are our link to the future and they must be nurtured, respected, loved, protected and educated.

9. That the unified Black family is the vital building block of the nation.

The Hedgehog Concept (The Build Allah Square)

1. Eat, Train, Read, Write, and Share

The Core Concepts

1. Black divinity, Black revolutionism, Black eroticism, Black astralism, Black demodernisation, and Black syndicalism

The Physical Concepts

1. biophysics, quantum physics, molecular physics, geophysics, astrophysics, and digital physics

The Discursive Concepts

1. body, embody, and disembody

2. structure, infrastructure, and superstructure

3. subtle, subaltern, and subterranean

4. text, pretext, subtext, and context

5. discourse, discursive, pre-discursive, narrative, and performative

6. reality, surreality, sub-reality, hyper-reality, virtual-reality, and unreality

7. erase, absent, present, represent, reproduce, re-enact, legitimate, and counter

8. position, supposition, disposition, composition, superposition, opposition, exposition, and imposition

9. silence, distort, fabricate, exaggerate, implicate, explicate, delineate, propagate, and voice

The Chronological Concepts

1. historicism and historicity

2. linear-chronological and event-sequential

3. historical, ahistorical, prehistorical, and transhistorical

The Pneumatological Concepts

1. demonise and transfigure

2. divine, vampyre, and devil

3. elemental, environmental, and universal

4. foresight, insight, and hindsight

5. *Sebi*, *Nebi*, and *Obi*

6. astral, astral body, astral force, and astral plane

7. *Hakim*, *Karim*, *Rahim*, and Allah

8. Horu construct, Hethor construct, Ausar conscious, and Auset conscious

9. existent, pre-existent, co-existent, de-existent, and re-existent

10. resurrected, incorporated, *phantomised*, internalised, and exorcised

11. empathic, psychopathic, sociopathic, *monopathic, duopathic, polypathic*, and *panopathic*

12. empath, dark empath, supernova empath, true empath, quiet empath, psychic empath, super empath, sigma empath, and Heyoka empath

The Psychological Concepts

1. conscious and unconscious

2. libido and superego

3. inhibition, prohibition, and exhibitionism

4. object, selfobject, and objectify

5. subject, subjective, and intersubjective

6. trauma, complex, and therapy

7. power, empower, internalise, incorporate, and concretise

8. spectre, drive, constraint, ideal, and somatic

The Ideological Concepts

1. seduction, perverse seduction, and seductionism

2. sexualise, racialise, and criminalise

3. White superiority, White supremacy, and White privilege

4. acculturate, assimilate, integrate, and institutionalise

5. gaze, oppress, problematise, and deviate

6. shackling, unshackling, deshackling, and reshackling

7. typical, atypical, prototypical, and archetypal

8. institution, destitution, restitution, constitution, deconstitution, and reconstitution

9. sexual, asexual, heterosexual, homosexual, transsexual, intersexual, and hypersexual

10. modern, premodern, postmodern, late modern (liquid modern), anti-modern, and demodernise

11. colony, market-colony, industrial-colony, military-colony, penal-colony, settler-colony, spatial-colony, cultural-colony, corporeal-colony, mental-colony, epistemic-colony, counter-colony, neo-colony, and the Great United States Empire (GUSE)

The Sociological Concepts

1. embodied displacement (exile, migration, trans-migration, or tourism) and disembodied displacement (phantasy, fantasy, wish, dream, vision, imagination, or astral journey)

2. aetiology, teleology, and eschatology

3. locality, globality, and communality

4. ordination, subordination, and superordination

5. gnosis, prognosis, diagnosis, and epignosis

6. inertia, action, interaction (force), and act-species

7. interior, exterior, anterior, posterior, and ulterior

8. mechanic, elastic, static, kinetic, dynamic

9. politics, geopolitics, biopolitics, necropolitics, transpolitics, hyper-politics, body-politics, racial-politics, and sexual-politics

The Sociological Axioms

1. The Axioms of Social Mechanics

a) $x > 1$

b) $v < 670{,}616{,}629$ mph

c) $v = \dfrac{d}{t}$

2. The Axioms of Social Force

a) $v\left(\dfrac{x^n}{x^n}\right) = \alpha$

b) $x_1 + R = Lm$ and $x_2 + S = Lm$

c) $\alpha > x^{10}$

3. The Axioms of Social Movements

a) $x_1 > x_2 \leftrightarrow x_2\alpha \searrow o$

b) $g \propto \alpha$

c) $g_1(pa) \rightarrow g_2(na)$ and $g_1(na) \rightarrow g_2(pa)$

d) $d = (2\pi) \times \left(\frac{2\lambda + 2A}{2}\right)$

4. The Axioms of Social Kinetics

a) $x_1 + x_2 \rightarrow na$

b) $x_1 + x_2 \rightarrow pa \leftrightarrow Lm \searrow$

c) $pa > Lm \rightarrow D \leftrightarrow pa \searrow$

5. The Axioms of Social Statics

a) $g(Lm) \leftrightarrow \alpha \searrow o$

b) $\exists \alpha \searrow o \rightarrow x^u \geq g$

6. The Axioms of Social Dynamics

a) $Lm > g$

b) $\exists(\alpha > Lm) \rightarrow g \nearrow$

c) $\exists Lm \rightarrow \alpha \searrow + g \searrow$

Preface of Book

The book you are about to read focuses primarily on presenting to the reader the depths of certain godbody structures and ideas, using *observant participation* (Wacquant 2008) as its primary source. In particular it centres on godbody lessons that I learned during my experiences in both Brooklyn, New York and London, England, and the guidance I was given from my mentor and enlightener within the godbody movement. A man who himself is currently doing time in prison for a crime he did not commit.

The book was also written as part of a much broader book, carrying with it the central purpose of representing the New York City street culture and revealing some of its remarkable ideas to the Black intelligentsia of America. However, as I found it ever more difficult to get a footing in this crowd and among this audience I decided to rethink my original plan. Finding instead a home among African professionals I considered it far more necessary to remove some of the more immature and gang related themes of the original content and repackage it as a theology. My main objective at this time, at least with the current endeavour, is now to expound in detail the various aspects of this unique ghetto movement. A movement that has created a cultural mechanism so effective that it has changed the face and shape of the ghetto youth of the American East Coast and Black American underclass to this very day.

Obviously this particular book does not speak for the entire movement that I belong to, nor does it attempt to, however, its aim is to present the relevant ideas articulated within the movement as given to me by my Sun and Enlightener God Born Supreme Allah as a means of creating a dialogue between the intellectuals of the godbody movement, and the intellectuals of the Black bourgeoisie. This could potentially allow the godbody to gain a level of acceptance, at least in intellectual circles, as a truly credible movement with a credible interpretation of theology, ideology, and sociology. Indeed, the Adamology to be presented in the following chapters show a clear identification with Islamic themes, or what has been called by myself anarcho-Islamism. It is, nevertheless, only Islamist in the sense of being based on a revolutionary Islam, not in the sense of being terroristic — as most godbodies themselves are anti-terrorism.

General Introduction

The ideology of the godbody is derived from the history of the Black struggle translated through theocentric-monism. Though we godbodies have a duty to bring knowledge of self to those who are uncivilised we are not tied down to any specific doctrine: what is demanded of us from the godbody elders (the older Gods and Goddesses) is to remember that the God of the Scriptures, whatever holy book it may be, is self and kind. As Black men we are God and our Black women are Goddesses: and though we Black people happen to currently be going through our psychological Dark Ages – we have not been able to channel our spiritual excellence into psychological empowerment – our destiny is to divinity.

However, to reach this goal there are several battles to be won along the way. Our first battle within this eschatological judgment is the Battle of Tel Megiddon (our Islamist Struggle). Our second battle within this eschatological judgment is the Battle of Divine Parousia (our Black Divinity Struggle). Our third battle within this eschatological judgment is the Battle of Sensual Resurrection (our Black Erotica Struggle). Our fourth battle within this eschatological judgment is the Battle of Cultural Enrapturement (our Black Astralist Struggle). Our fifth battle within this eschatological judgment is the Battle of

Anti-Capitalism (our Black Syndicalist Struggle). Finally, our sixth battle within this eschatological judgment is the Battle of Anti-Modernism (our Black Thearchist Struggle).

It all begins with a decision, but to paraphrase Cone, it is not a question of whether the Islamists are willing to die for their cause. We have more than enough proof of that. The question is whether the Jews and the Christians are willing to commit the genocide necessary to stop them from achieving their liberation. Unfortunately, we have been getting a blatantly clear answer to this question too. These birthing pangs being experienced in their struggles to achieve their liberation are merely the norm of most social movements or perspectives on their way to self-identity and self-expression. The godbody identity as an anarcho-Islamist movement is novel, however, it is also apt, as we, like the Islamists, see Islam as a way of life, and not merely as a religion.

With all this in mind, we godbodies also intend to inflict the wrath of Allah on all those who *oppose* our said way of life; acknowledging that a spirit of demonisation will be unleashed against our chosen way of living. Though it is likely that this could reverberate into the classic racial Manichaeism of the Black devil/White devil theory, we of the Black thearchy have expanded our understanding of evil to the causal and mental realms. It is here that we recognise the reality of *Shaitan* (Arabic for ethical, legal, and military adversity, or even for an omnimalevolent rage though better translated as an opposing one) as a force that will be locked in an epic Battle of Tel Megiddon with those of us godbodies that stand with Islamism, and in particular with Palestine in their own struggle for liberation, using trick knowledge and false signs to deceive the ignorant peoples of the world against us.

Notwithstanding, as the kingdom of Allah is supposed to be within us, to truly bring about the actual kingdom of Allah, or, in our case, a Black thearchy, we must, first of all, have a mental revolution. This mental revolution will also continue on until it effectively ends at our own personal Battle of Tel Megiddon when either the true Messiah crushes the Great *Dajjal*, or it ends at what could only be called the mental counter-revolution of the Great *Dajjal* acculturating and colonising a further mind to be added to his own army of persecutors for the godbody movement, and for Islam in general. These mentally acculturated and colonised soldiers for the Great *Dajjal* (Iblis) will thus be those who harass and persecute godbodyism in all its forms and side with Zionism in its effort to completely eradicate Islamism from the world, and the Islamic presence from the land of Palestine.

Yet in spite of the individually experienced tribulations we may go through as a result of our support for Palestine Allah will provide the godbodies with a little help. This will mainly be in the form of possessing the ability to interact with astral forces. This should also make us prone to entering into what is called in Islam a "state." While such may be all good and well we would in fact be much better off attaining to what is also called in Islam a "station." States are entered into through assistance from the astral plane, yet, even so, they operate by law. There are, at the same time, those that can attain supersensory abilities excessively easily: that includes astral seeing, hearing/speaking, smelling, tasting, and feeling/influencing. Abilities like these, however, only become easy for those who have the hereditary genealogy to master them. In this case, their genes, based on their specific family origin, determines their level of supersensory capacity. These levels of capacity do and will also get passed down in their genes.

As for evolution and mutation, such are processes that take hundreds of thousands of years. Thus, for our generation heredity is the best way for one to acquire access to supersensory abilities and pass them down to their seeds. Again, with regard to melination, it definitely is and will be very useful and helpful for the gaining and mastery of astral sensation, especially as astral sensation is acquired through the pineal gland. See, the pineal gland contains melatonin which produces dreams, visions, and astral perception. The pineal gland also has melanin (black pigmentation), meaning the melinated have a much greater possibility of accessing astral or supersensory perception.

As melination and having melination are the best ways to gain access to the astral plane (which includes astral/remote influencing, astral/remote seeing, astral/remote hearing/ speaking, astral smelling, and astral tasting) for the time being both heredity and melination will remain the best ways to attain to supersensory abilities. The hereditarily supersensory will obviously be more gifted/powerful than the simply melinated, however, if a melinated person were to study and learn to unlock the deeper levels of the supersensory then they will definitely supersede the hereditary owner of supersensory gifts who, at the same time, has no idea how to access their own genetic advantage.

It is education that gives one greater knowledge of the astral plane, but it is nothing if you cannot see or interact with the astral forces of the astral plane (or if they have no desire to interact with you). As noted, the two ways to see and interact in the astral plane are: (i) to enter into a state and (ii) to unlock the third eye of the pineal gland, and thus begin to rise up the various stations. These stations are: *Hakim* (Arabic for foresight, insight, and hindsight user, or even for a wise one; though better translated as an omnivisionary sage), which means becoming a master of the science of life. *Karim* (Arabic for clairvoyance, clairaudience, and clairsentience user, or even for a noble one; though better translated as an omnipotent mage), which means becoming a master of the Supreme Mathematics. *Rahim* (Arabic for climateopathic, biopathic, and panopathic user, or even for an empathic one; though better translated as an omnipresent hage), which means becoming a master of the Build Allah Square. *Allah* (Arabic for omnivisionary, omnipotent, and omnipresent deity, or even for a Supreme Being; though better translated as a divine one), which means becoming a grandmaster of the science of life, Supreme Mathematics, and the Build Allah Square.

As for those who seek to master plus degrees like *panopathy*, not everybody is able to develop those skills. For the most part, most of us will have to settle for some form of *polypathy*, maybe, for example, *climateopathy* (the non-coercive ability to communicate with and influence the elements), zoopathy (the non-coercive ability to communicate with and influence the animals), or maybe *cosmopathy* (the non-coercive ability to communicate with and warp time-space allowing for telekinesis, teleportation, and levitation throughout the cosmos). We gain these kinds of empathic abilities through understanding the deeps of the godbody lessons. Again, to most godbodies, such hocus pocus is only considered plus degrees, if that. To these godbodies, it is only by rising through the four stations of divinity that a Black person becomes God or Goddess, and better equipped to face all of *Shaitan's* devils and whatever vicious attacks they try to hurt us with.

What the Black thearchy does is combine these godbody lessons with the system of Black syndicalism. The godbody on their own have a kind of Paradise, we just need a working socio-economic programme. However, psychologically and philosophically we have reached into the heavens and made

Allah more real. It was written by the apostle John, "That which was from the beginning, which we have heard, which we have seen with our eyes, which we have looked upon, and our hands have handled, of the Word of life;" for by the Word becoming audible, visible, and tangible it allowed we flesh and blood human beings to acquiesce to its guidance.

Herein is found doctrine in which the Messiah provides us with a direct source to Black thearchism: he himself was washed with water, he a preacher to the poor, he himself was sexually ethical, he himself had a Lenten retreat, he a martyr and a beaten up penitent, and he the founder of both the Agape Feasts and the forgiveness of sins. This would also prove to be that example to all we who came after him. Again, you are not obliged to follow any of the rules or ideas of the godbody if you are not a member (neither will you be obliged to receive any of its many benefits). And though all this does put us in danger of becoming like our predecessors, at least for this millennium we will have Rapture being what could be called a communion of poor righteous teachers.

The Hunt for a Black Ramadan

In the early 1990s Samuel Huntington arrived at a general thesis that civilisations would clash. Now while I agree to an extent I do not see the future fault lines of the world being between his fictitious civilisations (some of which were quite ridiculous) but between Islam and *Ishrik* (polytheism). In this, where Huntington spoke of the Iron Curtain being replaced by a Velvet Curtain, I prefer the term Silk Curtain for three reasons: First, it employs the old Orientalist signifiers of what one imagines of the Orient – close to the imaginative and fictitious geographical and geopolitical ideas the West has of Islam. Second, there is a pre-modern, candidly ancient referential with regard to silk – even as the division between West and East travels as far back as Philip and Alexander, and even further back to ancient Sparta and ancient Persia. Third, silk, as opposed to velvet, is light, sometimes even transparent, thus it can go unnoticed with an almost invisible, unconscious air to it – even as the boundaries demarcating and segregating the Muslims from the *Mushriks* are light, invisible, and somewhat flimsy.

It is therefore not a clash of civilisations as such: according to the Prophet Islam has always been in the world, and even the forces of nature and of the universe are in perfect Islam. If Islam is the distinguishing characteristic of the universe, there is therefore a need to articulate various propositions and suppositions with the Islamic derivation that actually enumerate the eidetic intentionality of Islam and its correlation to Western religious and scientific perceptions.

Shari'ati spoke of a powerful consideration that is very important to Islam, the consideration of knowledge: "A person's character may be judged in accordance with his degree of knowledge concerning his beliefs, for the mere holding of a belief is no virtue in itself. If we believe in something that we do not fully know, it has little value. It is the precise knowledge of that in which we believe that may be counted a virtue. Since we believe in Islam, we must acquire correct knowledge of it and choose the correct method of gaining that knowledge" (Shari'ati 1979: 60). Indeed, most godbodies would say that belief should be excised from our vocabulary and mentality entirely. A person should be guided only by what they *know for sure*. Therefore, knowledge of Islam, more so than belief in Islam, should be what we endeavour to achieve.

Shari'ati articulated a central means to acquiring knowledge of Islam, making clear that his scientific method of developing a knowledge of Islam can be used to develop a knowledge of any religion or culture in society: "[T]here are various ways of knowledge of Islam. One is the knowledge of Allah, and comparing Him with the objects of worship in other religions. Another is the knowledge of our book, the Qur'an, and comparing it with other heavenly books (or books that are said to be heavenly). Yet another is the knowledge of the personality of the Prophet of Islam and comparing him with the great reforming personalities that have existed throughout history. Finally, one more is the knowledge of the outstanding personalities of Islam and comparing them with the prominent figures of other religions and schools of thought" (Shari'ati 1979: 42).

Now there is an essential apperception that must be acknowledged about Islam before we proceed any further: there is a distinction between identified Muslims and pious Muslims. Muslims in general have five basic indicators while pious Muslims have five different indicators. The five indicators that someone is an identified Muslim are belief in a beneficent and merciful God (*Allah*), belief in the oneness of God (*Tawhid*), belief in all the prophets of God from Adam to Muhammad (*Nubuwwa*), belief in the peace and harmony of the universe (*Islam*), and belief that every Muslim is a brother or sister Muslim (*Umma*). The five indicators of a pious Muslim are testifying to the oneness of God and the prophethood of Muhammad (*shahadah*); praying five times a day (*salah*); giving a portion of what you earn to those in need (*zakah*); fasting during the month of Ramadan (*sawm*); and going on the pilgrimage to Mecca when you have the means to do so (*hajj*). This essential apperception shows that the category of Muslim is far richer than simply the pious brand that most people acknowledge as our representatives.

Furthermore, as most experienced Muslims understand the depth of the *tawhidic* revelation is found in the *shahadah: La ilaha il Allah* (No god; but God). A statement that starts out with a negation (*nafy*) then it negates the negation with a counter-affirmation (*ithbat*). The *nafy* is of *shirk* (multiplicity), then it makes the *ithbat* of Allah's presence, that is, of Allah's existence. How a godbody would interpret this verse is — there is no mystery god; but Allah, the Supreme Being Black man from Asia, is the true and living God. As that is a mouthful most godbodies either say the *shahadah* or simply say "there is no mystery god."

As can be seen, we godbodies have our own *shahadah*, but we also have our own Mecca to which we all *hajj*, many of us practice *sawm* during Ramadan, we give a kind of *zakah* to those godbodies in need, and as far as *salah* goes, though we do not pray, let alone five times a day, it is written in the Quran, "Recite that which has been revealed to thee of the Book and keep up prayer. Surely prayer keeps (one) away from indecency and evil; and certainly the remembrance [*dhikr*] of Allah is the greatest ... And Allah knows what you do" (Quran 29: 45). Now this *dhikr* is in fact the Arabic word for meditation or mindfulness, and *al-dhikr* Allah is Arabic for the mindfulness of Allah. As the Quran says this mindfulness of Allah is of greater value than prayer (regardless of the amount of times a day it is done), those godbodies that practice mindfulness of Allah regularly, and many of us do, are actually in a greater position Islamically. In that sense, we godbodies can also be classified as pious Muslims, though we godbodies actually reject religious labels and would rather be called cultural Muslims.

But we can also gain a greater intimacy with the depths of Islam, which we do claim as our culture and way of life, through following Shari'ati's list. In so doing an overtly presented conclusion can be deduced immediately that Daulatzai captured when he said "God – via Christianity – came to be associated not only with whiteness but also with the powerful imperialist aggressor of the Western world, including the United States. Allah – via Islam – however, was 'out of power' and understood as Black." Shari'ati also concluded that what demarcated all the Abrahamic prophets from the non-Abrahamic prophets was that their missions and their systems were usually anti-establishment and "out of power," sometimes even to the point of invoking war and martyrdom. As Islam is the seal of the Abrahamic faiths it is only right that the God of Islam be an anti-establishment and anti-imperialist God. In all, the first thing we know for sure about Islam is that the God of Islam, Allah, is a God for the non-established.

"As for the book of Islam, the Qur'an, it is a book that like the Torah contains social, political and military provisions, even instructions for the conduct of warfare, the taking and setting free of prisoners; that is interested in life, in building, and prosperity, in struggling against enemies and negative elements; but it is also a book that concerns itself with the refinement of the soul, the piety of the spirit, and the ethical improvement of the individual" (Shari'ati 1979: 80). Ultimately, we can see conclusively therefore that the perspective of Islam is defined based on the book of Islam and the God of Islam.

In turn it can be perceived that the book of Islam is a book that comprises information about how to live in the world here and how to improve oneself for the world hereafter, and that the God of Islam is a God of the non-established, and particularly of Black, people. Yet Islamic history begins with the knowledge of this God and what sort of people he works with. According to Shari'ati he works with the prophets to send a message to the people. Moreover, "Prophets were individuals who transformed history and societies and they revolted as well as fomented a revolution. Who was Abraham? He was neither a philosopher nor a scientist. His father made idols and he would sell them. Later, he became a shepherd and finally he led the greatest movement in history. Or, look at Moses, he was an abandoned child who was brought up in Pharaoh's Palace. He took off and went to Shoeyb and began to herd his sheep. Finally, he started his struggles with Pharaoh with his gnarled staff and he won! The same is true about Jesus, Muhammad, and all the Prophets" (Shari'ati 1981: 2058).

The personages of Islamic history: the prophets, caliphs, and Imams, all trace their lineage back to Abraham, and, as can be seen, served a non-pretentious and non-established deity. Indeed, it is when their movements became the establishment that Islam would historically begin to fall. We see this throughout Islamic history, however, we learn just as much by studying the book of Islam: the Quran. Therefore, what we have learned about the God of Islam is that he is an anti-establishment, anti-imperialist, and anti-pretentious God. We learn the same also by studying the history of Islam and the personalities of Islam: from Abraham, to Moses, to Jesus and Muhammad, to the caliphs and the Imams.

But we do not learn completely the place and identity of man in the plan of Islam. From here Shari'ati went on to ask a quite pertinent question, "Can we deduce the status and nature of man from the manner in which the creation of man is described in the Qur'an, the Word of God, or in the words of the Prophet of Islam? From examining the story of Adam – the symbol of man – in the Qur'an, we can understand what kind of a creature man is in the view of God and therefore in the view of our religion" (Shari'ati 1979: 71). It will thereby be through the Quran that we will learn the true Islamic philosophy of man.

Moreover, in the Muslim internationalism of Shari'ati the *umma* is the societal manifestation of this philosophy of man. Basically, one can automatically join the *umma* or Muslim International by living out the practices of the Quran. But *umma* is more than simply the living out the Islamic philosophy of man, *umma*, according to Shari'ati has a functional, pretty much teleological, definition about it. "The word *umma* derives from the root *amm*, which has the sense of path and intention. The *umma* is, therefore, a society in which a number of individuals, possessing a common faith and goal, come together in harmony with the intention of advancing and moving towards the common goal." The immanent intentionality presumed therefrom commits the *umma* to a teleological definition as opposed to a spatial orientation. It is in all ways a noetic correlate, particularly with regard to forces.

Godbodyism and Adamology

Now the first and most important detail the Quran teaches us about man (and I use the masculine not to undermine women but to make the distinction) is that he was created by, and therefore must be subservient to, Allah: "Allah is the Creator of all things and He has charge over everything" (Quran 39: 62). The world and everything we know was created by Allah and for a purpose; though there is categorically some teleological significance in that idea it is not to say that Allah does not allow the world a measure of agency. If the world did not have any agentic capacities then all beings would be merely automatons doing the will of Allah not by choice but by necessity. That said, Allah has nonetheless also appointed for everything in the universe its measure, as it is written: "And there is not a thing but with Us are the treasures of it, and We send it not down but in a known measure." And again, "He said: Our Lord is He Who gives to everything its creation, then guides (it). … He said: The knowledge thereof is with my Lord in a book; my Lord neither errs nor forgets –" (Quran 15: 21; 20: 50-52). The Quran thus teaches us that Allah set and knows the limits of all things in the world.

Nevertheless, there is an ultimate question that arises from the understanding, according to the book of Islam, that man was created by Allah and was appointed by structures that he set in place natural limitations he could not transgress: In what way was man created when Allah created Adam? It is written, "And surely We created man of sounding clay, of black mud fashioned into shape" (Quran 15: 26); a proposition made no less evident by the discovery of the earliest fossils of humanity in East Africa. Again, the original Eden was most likely a savannah in East Africa and not an astral garden in the netherworld (Muller 2013). Here the evidence of the Quran and modern science agree that humanity's origin is as Black and that Adam or the Original man was fashioned from minerals in the African soil.

Indeed, virtually all the elements of our planet are found in the human body, though the elemental distributions may vary. Again, the most plenteous minerals of the earth are in brown or black colours and rarely, if at all, in pink or white. If Adam was made from black mud fashioned like clay into a human body – the story is an analogy – he would have had to have been Black. Yet it also says of him that he was created from dust, "When thy Lord said to the angels: Surely I am going to create a mortal from dust. So when I have made him complete and breathed into him of My spirit, fall down submitting to him" (Quran 38: 71, 72). Two implications can be drawn from these statements: (i) the spirit of Allah has always dwelt within man, (ii) "All the angels of God, great and small, are commanded to fall down in prostration before this creature" (Shari'ati 1979: 75).

Thereby what we can see is that in Islamic sociology: (i) Allah created all things, including Adam; (ii) Allah created Adam from dust and black mud; (iii) Allah breathed into Adam "not His blood or His body – so to speak – but His spirit, the most exalted entity for which human languages possess a name" (Shari'ati 1979: 74). The duality by which humanity is composed is based on being in a sense a dual nature: divine and profane. Man, however, is not distinguished by this duality: every creature has the breath of life; and while Shari'ati reasoned that humanity's "splendor and importance derive precisely from [this]" (Shari'ati 1979: 74), such is not the case.

In Genesis it says "And they went in onto Noah into the ark, two and two of all flesh, wherein is the breath of life" (Genesis 7: 15); and though I recognise the analogous nature of the Noah narrative – that the species of animals are too numerous and diverse to have fit into a literal ark, and that the existence of Noah himself may be questionable – that is beside the point. The point is that all creatures and species contain the breath of life not just humanity. Indeed, the breath of life or spirit of Allah flows throughout nature. Yet as we saw, the angels of Allah were also commanded to bow before Adam: "This prostration of the angels before Adam serves to clarify the Islamic concept of man. Man knows certain things that the angels do not know, and this knowledge endows man with superiority to the angels despite the superiority of the angels to man with respect to race and origin. In other words, the nobility and dignity of man derives from knowledge and not from lineage" (Shari'ati 1979: 75). In fact, as I shall try to prove later on, what distinguishes humanity as a species is knowledge.

The Quran also teaches that the woman was also made by Allah in similitude to man, "And Allah has made wives for you from among yourselves, and has given you sons and daughters from your wives, and has provided you with good things. Will they then believe in falsehood and deny the favour of Allah?" (Quran 16: 72). Incidentally, to refine our understanding of this exegetic text Shari'ati articulated, "Another point to be considered is the creation of woman from the rib of man, at least according to the translations usually made from the Arabic. But the translation 'rib' is incorrect, and the word so translated has the real meaning, in both Arabic and Hebrew, of 'nature, disposition or constitution.' Eve – that is, woman – was created, then, out of the same nature or disposition as man." What is remarkable is that it was translated as rib in the first place, the idea of man's dual nature of divinity and profanity being embodied in a female of the same physical and sensual constitution, but with certain composite biological distinctions: chromosomes, hormones, breasts, vaginas, wombs, and ova; shows a greater depth than mythological ideation. It is the basis of our relation to the world and to Allah who created the world.

At the same time, I must say at this point that contrary to popular opinion I am sympathetic towards the ideology of feminism, particularly pro-sex feminism, and by no means hope to eradicate it. However, there is an issue within their theoretical propositions that might be preventing their progression as a movement in the future: there is a tendency among some feminists to use the concept of man for an idealised evil. To say that all the problems of women, if not of the world, are a result of men. Men become the absolute oppressor, manipulator, tempter, or womaniser. In this case, the essentialised become the essentialisers.

Even when done from an historical perspective, so as to point out male-centred/male-created structures, it is done so with the absolutised evil men deceiving the idealisation of an absolutely innocent – and just as historically constructed – version of the feminine, for example, in de Beauvoir's statement, among many, that "Lord-man will materially protect liege-woman and will be in charge of justifying her existence: [so that] along with the economic risk, she eludes the metaphysical risk of a freedom that must invent its goals without help" (de Beauvoir 2009: 10). There is a danger here of essentialising all men under the position of absolute corrupter/deceiver without respecting the power dynamics of the time.

Also there is kind of a feeling that many of these feminists have a "cut off your nose to spite your face" mentality. They hate men so much that they have no desire to see or produce any benefit for them at all. What do I mean by this? I have heard women say that they do not want sexual liberation because men benefit from it. The way I see it, that would be like a slave saying they do not want emancipation because the slavemaster benefits more than the slaves. You may as, in what ways? They no longer need to preserve and protect the slaves. They no longer need to feed, house, and clothe them. They no longer need to pay for ownership of them. They no longer need to pay exorbitant fire insurance prices. They are no longer condemned by the North as slaveholders, et cetera. These benefits may have accrued to the former slaveholder but, man, would they rather have maintained slavery. Same with female sexual confidence, polyamory, sensual freedom, light exhibitionism, seductionism, and hypereroticism. Though obviously men gain certain small benefits from these and women gain only one: like with slave emancipation that one is so big that it trumps the gains men get. Herein, I see the anti-sex feminists as those who are trying to cut off their nose to spite their faces.

Again, it is not that the pro-sex women become like men, they actually become more dangerous and more powerful than men. These women are able to become an obsession for the men. Men will buckle, bend, and break over a woman who is genuinely emancipated sexually as such a woman is so rare. Saying, such a woman is a "pick me" or other such things obscures her reality. She is playing a role to seduce a man she wants that night, first of all. Second, she is polyamorous so she has no need of this particular man or any other. Third, as Napoleon Hill said, "One of America's most able businessmen frankly admitted that his attractive secretary was responsible for most of the plans he created. He confessed that her presence lifted him to heights of creative imagination, such as he could experience under no other stimulus" (Hill 2004: 217). The reason the concept of the muse is usually feminine is because only women can inspire with such depth. The idea that men are sexual gods is foolish when women have the potential to be far superior to us in sexuality. Far superior to us.

So, as godbodies we must now ask: Why have certain ideas become so widespread within certain social bodies, and what will be the circumstances of their development or decay? If all that is considered is the failings of a particular section of a social body or the constructing of a group as absolute failure/evil as a reverse of having been constructed or marginalised by them as inferior, then the most that can occur is a reversal of circumstances where the oppressed become the oppressors of their former oppressors (like Marx's expropriation of the expropriators). Such may seem fitting but it will not be as fulfilling as hoped, it will inevitably only create an insatiable lust for more power until the pendulum swings back in favour of the former oppressors.

Furthermore, as the Quran continued, humanity's rebellion against Islam began with both Adam and Eve, saying: "But the devil made them [Adam and Eve] slip from it, and caused them to depart from the state in which they were. And We said: Go forth, some of you are the enemies of others. And there is for you in the earth an abode and a provision for a time. Then Adam received (revealed) words from his Lord, and He turned to him (mercifully). Surely He is Oft-returning (to mercy), the Merciful" (Quran 2: 36, 37). Remember, these were two Black people. The symbolic and figurative nature of the story does not diminish the value of this understanding. Conversely, Adam fell from Islam because of the devil, Adam rose back to Islam because of Allah's mercy.

This is a central distinction between the Islamic philosophy of man and the Christian. In Christianity humanity is born wicked because of Adam's sin and needs the coming of Jesus to be saved, in Islam Adam's sin affects only Adam and only for a brief moment until Allah forgives him, therefore humanity is neither born wicked nor in need of a saviour. The Messiah came to redeem humanity from open rebellion to Allah, but such was a result of the devils' corrupting each of us individually through *shirk*. What the godbody perspective does is it exorcises the mysticism from Islam: a Muslim becomes simply anyone who believes in and teaches *tawhid* and a *Mushrik* becomes anyone who believes in and teaches *shirk* (multiplicity).

Nevertheless, as the purpose of the Adamic analogy was to explain to new generations that the Original people were Black people created by Allah in his own image, that also puts a twist to the Noah analogy too, where it says, "And it came to pass, when men began to multiply on the face of the earth, and daughters were born unto them, That the sons of God saw the daughters of man that they were fair [in Hebrew *towb*, literally meaning good, that is, good to look at, beautiful]; and they took them wives of all which they chose" (Genesis 6: 1, 2). If Adam was an Asiatic Black man then the daughters of Adam would have been beautiful Asiatic Black women, women that looked so good that even the angels were unable to resist them. In fact, in my opinion Allah only created the Black woman to show off.

The Beauties of Libido

On a deeper level, what all the above Scriptures are saying is what certain schools of psychology also teach: that mindfulness (*dhikr*) of the Lover (al-Muhibb) can lead one into Paradise. While this conclusion is itself charged with affectivity, identifying its scientific externalities requires us to look deeper into psychology – and ultimately into the ontology of nature – before we can continue on articulating the variations within Black thearchism.

In psychological study it is imperative to first choose a perspective from which to make our analysis. Within Black thearchism it is the perspectives of depth psychology: in particular those of Freud and Adler; therefore if we hope to go any further in the Black thearchic perspective it will be necessary to receive a brief grounding in Freudian and Adlerian theory and how they interconnect. To begin with, Freud saw all affectivity as discharges of sexual energy, that being the basis of how a person related to the world exterior to them. "For Freud, a person's interest in the world is a manifestation of his investing it with sexual energy, which he called *libido*. The world's ceasing to exist for a person and his withdrawal of libido from the world are, for Freud, two aspects of the same process" (Lear 1998: 133). Or basically, "The world exists because we invest it with sexual energy" (Lear 1984; quoted in Lear 1998: 140).

Lear could make such a statement based on his understanding of Freudian analysis, particularly of "primary narcissism" the state by which libido is invested in the self to create a self-identity, that is, primordial ego. However, the libido has an even greater personification within Black thearchism. Thereby the libidinal becomes the divine, which is based on the very essence of Allah, the *Dhatullah*. Moreover, within Black thearchism the *Dhatullah* is based on the combining of three Greek concepts that are personified in the libido: the erotic, the agapic, and the empathic. However, in Freudian theory, not only is it also through libido that an infant begins to differentiate itself from the world; but it is also understood that the same libido is then invested back into the world by the infant as a manifestation of divinity. *Again, this thesis was not to propose some complicated infantile masturbatory theory or to promote some paedophilic stimulation, it was developed to explain human psychic development.*

To Freud the libido was the sexual energy formulated by the sexual drive. Though the root of sexual energy may be located in the erotogenous zones – like the root of the nervous system is located in the brain and the root of the circulatory system is located in the heart – the hormonal distributions aroused by the pleasant sensations are relational to the endocrine system. Moreover, the sexual drive itself, from whence the sexual energy derives, derives itself from the hypothalamic part of the brain. Obviously, to a prepubescent sexuality is an innocuous ideation; but that, however, does not negate the possibility of a prepubescent sexual drive. Again, "It seems probable that the sexual drive is in the first instance independent of its object; nor is its origin likely to be due to the object's attractions" (Freud 1981; quoted in Lear 1998).

The sexual drive is therefore independent of the sexual object it desires and so exists like other drives in the human body without any form of malicious or devious referent. As an example, even before we learned how to use the toilet we had a drive to urinate; even before we learned the usefulness of food to our bodies and our lives we had a drive to eat; and even before we learned how to use language we had a drive to be social. All these drives are improved by a family that invests love into the infant; the infant's response thus becomes clear, to invest libido back into the world it has come to differentiate from itself.

Sexual objectification is not necessarily a negative as such, at least in Freudian theory, investing sexual energy into something is to give it value, to internalise within the self that the object is meaningful. Interestingly, the discharge of sexual energy does not necessarily mean having sex with a sexual object, but simply agreeing that it is a pleasurable object, that it excites and stimulates your libido. "For a person to be able libidinally to invest in an object, the object must be something *for* the person. The object must have psychic reality. This must be true even when the 'object' is the [ego] or the self" (Lear 1998: 134). During the developmental process a parent's or family member's display of love nurtures the infant and creates their first sexual object. Because an infant has no idea what sex is they manifest their sexual desire through archaic dreams – at least in Freudian theory. This sexual energy soon gets internalised as the infant learns to differentiate its primordial ego from the world outside of itself.

Sexual energy can be discharged without the act of sex or masturbation ever taking place. Conversely, when the infant's sexual object becomes the self, such does not lead to infantile masturbatory self-stimulation but to primary narcissistic development. Freud also "insisted that a developing infant must experience frustration if he is ever to perceive an independently existing world. … And it is through all the frustrating descendants of [their] primal frustration that the world comes to have psychological reality for him" (Lear 1998: 157). For an infant to come to a point that they are able to differentiate themselves from an independently existing reality they have to go through a level of disappointment. They have to experience disappointment in order to develop the mental capacities, and the desire to develop the mental capacities, to overcome their disappointment.

This is a fundamental aspect of human development: the will, or as Freud called it, the death drive, and as Adler called it, the striving for power. It is the second product of the developmental process, even before the self-identity has been constructed and identified the striving for power is developed by the libido. This occurs usually when the object of the infant's affective desire is not immediately consumed by the infant, the frustration at trying to acquire or consume the object causes them to realise that they do not have the power to do whatsoever they want to do; their immediate response is a kind of inferiority feeling, which for the infant gets instantly translated into a striving for that power. All these affects – the frustration, the inferiority feeling, the perception of reality, the striving for power – occur at the speed of femtoseconds, making it impossible to decipher when one ends and the other begins.

Accordingly, Lear presented a complete summation of the developmental process of an infant: "At the beginning of life there are no firm boundaries between self and world, nor are there firm boundaries between wishing and reality. The newborn's wishes suffice his 'world.' Each recognition of the mother's separateness is by its nature also of frustration and disappointment. In response the mother is taken in, but so are the child's wishes! For where they once held sway over the world, they are now evermore confined to the interior of the child's developing soul." It is at this point that the infant's sexual energy goes from being invested purely externally to being invested internally and the infant's sexual object goes from being the mother to being the self, i.e. narcissism.

Significantly, during all succeeding instances of the now narcissistic sexual energy being invested into an external sexual object the boundaries of differentiation again get severely blurred. According to Freud, in most romantic relationships, "we see that the object is being treated in the same way as our own [ego], so that when we are in love a considerable amount of narcissistic libido overflows on to the object. It is even obvious in many forms of love-choice that the object serves as a substitute for some unattained [superego] of our own" (Freud 1981; quoted in Lear 1998: 197). Thereby, sexual energy gets invested in the world outside of ourselves, outside of primary narcissistic libido, due to us seeing ourselves, whether our current selves or our ideal selves, in someone else.

The preceding ideas were all preliminary and necessary to fully understand and appreciate the Freudian system of developmental psychology, now we come to the crux of the matter. Libido or sexual energy is the central source of our affective disposition to the world, our sexual objects, being independent of our sexual drives, are malleable but when coupled with disappointment (or rejection) can cause mental interpretive developments of the similitude to our archaic mental developments. While in infancy the disappointment was advantageous in many ways, it is less so in adolescence and adulthood, and may even be traumatic. In either case, it will produce change.

When our sexual drive desires a sexual object that it cannot attain the consequences could be very substantial, "we libidinally invest the world and it comes to have reality for us. Were we to withdraw libidinal investment in the world, it would come to an end (for us)." The eschatological implications inherent in this statement impose a radical supposition: the End of the World – as well as any eschatological paradigm shifts – is an individually and socially experienced transition that occurs as a result of libidinal inhibition. Libido is thus a necessity if we are to avoid meaninglessness.

Consequently, Freud thus developed his libidinal theory into something all-encompassing:

> *"Libido is an expression taken from the theory of the emotions. We call by that name the energy, regarded as a quantitative magnitude (though not at present actually measurable), of those instincts which have to do with all that may be comprised under the word 'love.' The nucleus of what we mean by love naturally consists (and this is what is commonly called love, and what the poets sing of) in sexual love with sexual union as its aim. But we do not separate from this – what in any case has a share in the name 'love' – on the one hand, self-love, and on the other, love for parents and children, friendship and love for humanity in general, and also devotion to concrete objects and to abstract ideas. Our justification lies in the fact that psycho-analytic research has taught us that all these tendencies are an expression of the same instinctual impulses; in relations between the sexes these impulses force their way towards sexual union, but in other circumstances they are diverted from this aim or are prevented from reaching it, though always preserving enough of their original nature to keep their identity recognizable ..."*

Though sexual energy is the basis of libido the concept itself is far broader. Indeed, libido could in fact be considered a divine principle. Moreover, Allah's essence is considered to be libidinal within this Black thearchic theory. Further, the vast majority of social relations between individuals and the world could even be articulated as libidinal; it is only when we come to social bodies that we reach a point of competitive – possibly even conflictual – articulation. While a person may individually invest the world with sexual energy a social body initially invests the world with personal aggrandizement, every social body gives itself a personal mission – we godbodies being no different – to define the world. The social kinetics of in-group relations shows that though libidinal energy flows to the group and its members it is denied to out-group social bodies and individuals.

Such is the case because the stability of the social body is compromised by inter-group relations. Though not completely, sometimes there are alliances, unions, or mergers that transpire as a result of inter-group communication, such, however, is not the initial case and in the vast majority of inter-group relations the initial confrontation is usually hostile or non-hostile competition, each seeing itself as the superior social body. Once lines of communication are opened and offending systems and practices are removed or adjusted libidinal energy is then able to be transmitted to the second social body as to one's own. Such a transmission coincides with erotic agency as narcissistic libido can be coerced from a social body by erotic expropriation. Indeed, as Freud said, "in its origin, function, and relation to sexual love, the 'Eros' of the philosopher Plato coincides exactly with the love-force, the libido of psycho-analysis …"

If there is a Paradise in the universe then it is reached only through eroticism and its fulfilment is in orgasmic ecstasy. Erotic seduction is resoundingly affective and attracts the sexual drive, thereby blurring the boundaries of differentiation. As libido is coerced from the social body it effectively surrenders its offending qualities and attempts union with the second body. In both cases there is sacrifice and in both cases there is the expending of sexual energy, but the ultimate objective is inter-group unity and solidarity. Again, Lévi-Strauss theorised that the initial bond unifying the different tribes of antiquity was also sexual in nature, whether this is true or not, sexuality is capable of playing an effective, and, indeed, affective, role in removing the differentiation between out-groups and the in-group. Furthermore, as Lear stated, "if our tie to the world is genuinely erotic, we can no longer conceive the world as a mere receiver or inhibitor of our discharges. Love is not just a feeling or a discharge of energy, but an emotional orientation to the world." This thereby demonstrates that our ideas, ideologies, and perspectives of the world are determined, and can be changed, by our libidinal disposition.

While Freud's libido theory may have received heavy criticism: any truth that offends is a truth nonetheless. We can also see in it the substantiation of the Islamic belief that love, particularly the love between a man and a woman, is a sign from Allah. But humanity is not alone in possessing this kind of love, most mammals are both erotic and empathic. Indeed, according to Lear, Freud's theory of love "did not confine itself to the human soul; it was occurring throughout animate nature, even within a single living cell", thus reasoning that it transcends humanity and encompasses all organic life. There is no disagreement here with the Quran either, as it is written: "And there is no animal in the earth, nor a bird that flies on its two wings, but (they are) communities like yourselves. We have not neglected anything in the Book. Then to their Lord will they be gathered" (Quran 6: 38).

Basically, the breath of life of Genesis is not necessarily breath in the lungs, nor even in the nostrils – though such has been used in conjunction with the breath of life (the word for nostrils in Hebrew is *aph*, which can also mean face or forehead. This is interesting as the word translated as breath of life when it is usually used in conjunction with the word nostrils is *neshamah*, which actually means intellect or divine inspiration – as opposed to the word *ruakh*, which translates from the Hebrew as wind, breath, or spirit) – thus could in fact be very libido or libidinal energy.

The Power of Man

As we now see, the Islamic philosophy of man agrees in many ways with certain schools of scientific thought: (i) man has an organic relation to all living things which in essence contain a similar if not the same origin; (ii) the Original man was made of the same elements found in the earth; (iii) our earliest human ancestors were Black people; (iv) the forces of nature (angels) are able to be mastered by humanity; (v) humanity, like all organic nature, has the spirit of life, which is the libido; and (vi) when the libido is inhibited the world becomes meaningless. Returning now to the Quran we also find out that man was also given authority according to Quranic exegesis: "And when thy Lord said to the angels, I am going to place a ruler in the earth, they said: Wilt Thou place in it such as make mischief in it and shed blood? And we celebrate Thy praise and extol Thy holiness. He said: Surely I know what you know not." "And when We said to the angels, Be submissive to Adam, they submitted, but Iblis (did not). He refused and was proud, and he was one of the disbelievers" (Quran 2: 30, 34).

It is clear from these verses the eminence accorded to man by Allah in the Quran; as a result Islam sees man as the highest of Allah's creatures on the earth "a ruler in the earth" and as high also in the heavens "We said to the angels, Be submissive to Adam," even European humanism does not accord humanity so high a position. Again, the word translated in the verse above as ruler is the Arabic word *Khalifah*, which means successor, trustee, or viceregent. Therefore, "The same mission that God has in the cosmos, man must perform on the earth as God's viceregent. The first excellence that man possesses is, then, being God's representative on earth" (Shari'ati 1979: 73). The narrative of Adam, being an analogical symbol of humanity (Adam in both Hebraic and Arabic translates to Original humanity), imposes on common humanity the responsibility of trusteeship over the earth. In a sense, even from the origin Allah appointed Adam, and thereby the Original people, to be *darwishs* (poor, righteous, teachers), from whence we also get the term dervishs.

Moreover, Shari'ati believed that man was distinguished from all other creatures under the sun by three qualifiers: (i) the breath of life, (ii) the *Khalifah*, and (iii) the Trust that Allah gave to man (which he believed to be the ability to go against our instinctual nature). It is written in the Quran, "Surely We offered the trust to the heavens and the earth and the mountains, but they refused to be unfaithful to it and feared from it, and man has turned unfaithful to it. Surely he is ever unjust, ignorant" (Quran 33: 72). This trust that was given to man separates him from all things in heaven and on earth. However, as far as the ability to go against our instinctual nature, humanity is very instinctual, particularly in our affectivity, therefore I believe the trust is actually the *Khalifah*. So what actually distinguishes humanity from the animals in my opinion are three somewhat different qualifiers: (i) the *Khalifah* (which is our trusteeship), (ii) libidinal sublimation, and (iii) knowledge.

Perhaps the key attribute of man that separates him from all other species is knowledge. It is written, again, in the

Quran: "And He taught Adam all the names, then presented them to the angels; He said: Tell Me the names of those if you are right. They said: Glory be to Thee! we have no knowledge but that which Thou hast taught us. Surely Thou art the Knowing, the Wise. He said: O Adam, inform them of their names. So when he informed them of their names, He said: Did I not say to you that I know what is unseen in the heavens and the earth? And I know what you manifest and what you hide" (Quran 2: 31-33). Like with Durkheim and Mauss, the Quran agrees that what distinguishes humanity is our ability to classify and categorise. However, the godbody expand this conception to an internal striving for knowledge and a receptivity to know.

Basically, to us godbodies humanity has an interaction with knowledge unavailable to any other creature. Knowledge is the key to our evolution, once humanity began learning and mastering their surroundings they became truly human. In fact, Homo sapiens is Latin for the thinking man, even as Homo habilis is for the handy man, Homo ergaster is for the working man, and Homo erectus is for the upright man. The distinction of humanity from these earlier hominidae is thus our ability to acquire, develop, and apply knowledge. *Scientia* is the Latin for knowledge, yet scientific elevation does not negate human artistic capabilities.

The artistic and the cultural are just as unique to humanity as knowledge, though while other animals are capable of learning (e.g. horses, dogs, beavers, and mites) their ability to enact cultural performances is purely instinctual, even when they perform a transformative of nature it is based entirely on instinct. Humanity, on the other hand, performs cultural and technical works based only to some degree on instinct. What really occurs, according to Freud, is that the instincts, effectively the sexual drives, get sublimated into something more socially acceptable.

In this, all the activities, all the achievements, all the progresses that have been made by humanity are a result of a moral dilemma: the desire to have continual sexual relations in a world that condemns, or at least deplores, those that do. When a bee or a beaver builds their constructions they are following their illimited instinctual drive to do so; when a person builds an architectural feature or a work of art it is because they are sublimating their delimited instinctual drive. Consequently, as Lear said, "Our greatest cultural achievements, Freud speculated, may be due to [this] sublimation"; therefore, whereas it could be said that humanity possesses more knowledge and cultural genius than the other animals, humanity is not as autonomous or as uninhibited.

But if such is true of our cultural and technical narratives and performatives could it not also be true of all cultures in general? Are all human subcultures in fact just a sublimation of our instincts? If it is true then what is commonly considered the conscious mind is in fact a result of many generations of inhibitors – particularly European inhibitors – which have gained global credibility. Furthermore, the striving for power's elevation to the forefront of our conscious thinking is hereby shown to be the result of nothing more than the sublimation of our sexual energy.

The striving for power (which Freud called the death drive), according to Adler is the prerequisite of human psychological functioning, which is only beneficial so long as it is based upon the social interest. Adler, in his summation of psychological impetus, pointed out two potentially disconnected potentially interconnected drives in humanity, presenting his "evidence to show that the line of movement of human striving originates in the blending of social interest with the striving for personal superiority." These drives or motivations when they are interconnected influence a person toward socially progressive developments and are what I shall call the striving for empowerment.

Then again, as Adler continued, "In all problem people, excluding the feebleminded, we find that their goal of personal striving for power has miscarried but that all their movements are 'intelligent.' ... Accordingly they will lack the developed social interest and the courage which are necessary for the useful solution of the problems of life." When the striving for power takes place without the social interest to chase it it is no longer the striving for empowerment but the striving for personal superiority. Again, if the social interest is really just another name for the libido then there is actually shown here a gradation of libidinality within us.

The gradation system of the libido is a means of measuring an astral or social body's level of psychological stability, not based on normality, or what is considered normal by societal standards, but what the conscious and unconscious mind strive for. (i) At the highest the libido is enacted as sexual exhibitionism, thus the superego (or Ethos) becomes libidinal thereby allowing for the already libidinal instincts to have freedom of expression: at this level there could possibly even be the conscious or unconscious development of clairvoyance, clairsentience, clairaudience, or all three. (ii) When the libido has been sublimated by the striving for power then the astral forces of the individual or the social forces of the social group push them to strive for empowerment. (iii) When the striving for power begins to inhibit the libido then there is what Adler called the striving for personal superiority, which can manifest any one of these neurotic symptoms:

megalomania/superiority complex, depression/hypersensitivity, phobia/anxiety, or all three. (iv) At the final stage the inhibition is significant and the striving for power becomes prohibitive to the libido, at this time any one of these three symptoms of psychoses may become evident: delusions of grandeur, hallucinations, paranoia, or all three.

What transpires in the psychic figurations when different cultures are created is their libido usually gets sublimated and their striving for empowerment gets ameliorated, as this striving for empowerment usually means the empowerment of the social group, the cultural parameters of the social group become more defined along with the empowering of the subculture. It is written in the Scriptures concerning each subculture: "… For everyone of you We appointed a law and a way. And if Allah had pleased He would have made you a single people, but that He might try you in what He gave you. So vie one with another in virtuous deeds. To Allah you will all return, so He will inform you of that wherein you differed" (Quran 5: 48). Allah has thus appointed for each subculture its own structures and systems. Nevertheless, they are each based entirely on the level of striving for power. Low levels of this striving means they can focus on sexual emancipation, higher levels means the sexual drive of those in that subculture will be inhibited by it.

From Power to Supremacy

As future generations join a new culture they will learn to exhibit, inhibit, or sublimate their sexual drives within the social body so as to attain social acceptance. Whereby we can see that the first inhibition of human sexual energy must have been the establishment of the patriarchy. Not to buy into the whole social evolution theory, especially as it always seems to favour White culture over all non-White cultures – I speak here using the colonial definitions – but as one studies what we know of the pre-dynastic Egyptian and pre-dynastic Kushite cultures they were matriarchal long before they became patriarchal. If in fact the more ancient the culture the more matriarchal it was likely to be, then what took place to change that?

At this point an even more pertinent question would be, what is it that allowed the patriarchy, such a precarious and desultory form of governance, to maintain not only an existence but even a dominance in the world for so many thousands of years? Sexual inhibition to a certain degree answers that question. Although I cannot say I know the initial act that caused women to fall into subjection (and such has been an issue of debate since Europeans first discovered matrilineal tribes in the Americas) it is clear how the domination of women was maintained: by essentialising women as *nothing more than* sexual objects and then making sex and sexuality publicly taboo, thus men were able to prolong their domination over women. There are some obvious discrepancies though, a wife still has some influence over her husband – nevertheless, the dominance of man in general still proves the greater.

The inhibitive nature of the struggle of the sexes created the current repression of human libido. While the libido in itself is still the strongest force in all organic nature, including human nature; as the libido gets inhibited by Eurocentric trick knowledge, the striving for power innate within all human beings becomes the more dominant pursuit of conscious activity, diverting all the energies of our consciousness towards that end: in which case both inhibition and sublimation could be considered the cause of European industriousness and cultural achievement. Albeit thanks to Eurocentric trick knowledge the libido is now substantially inhibited, thus they cannot genuinely be called alive, or at least not living with meaning, as without libido life has no meaning.

Not only so, but with the libido now given indirect outlets, precarious narratives like that of pan-European distinction, and objectionable performatives like those of slavery, colonisation, segregation, and penalisation do and will manifest themselves more readily. That is not to say that all narratives are precarious or that all performatives are objectionable, just that while sexual sublimation may, on the one hand, be the cause of some of our greatest feats and triumphs; sexual inhibition and sexual repression could be the cause of some of our most unfortunate and unnecessary failures. All human systems may in fact be indirect exhibitions of human sexuality, therefore by deploring direct sexual exhibitionism, the social body, that is, the patriarchal social body, has created so many unnecessary systems and institutions. Very few systems have really been of any serious benefit to humanity thereby making most of them in a genuine sense meaningless.

Another interesting question arises from the matrix: what allows a social system to move beyond the transient and so perpetuate itself? The reason for this question should be evident to anyone who has been paying attention to what has been written so far: if the patriarchy, an obvious form of male-domination, has been able to endure for thousands of years virtually unchallenged with only minor pockets of matriarchal revival in some African, Native American, and pagan cultures, while on the whole, the world, including those very cultures, have only been getting more patriarchal, how do we keep White supremacy, an obvious form of White-domination, from also lasting thousands of years, while, at the same time, fighting against the patriarchy?

These issues are of great importance within Islam as it was commanded of Allah: "And fight [jihad] in the way of Allah against those who fight against you but be not aggressive. Surely Allah loves not the aggressors. And kill them wherever you find them, and drive them out from where they drove you out, and persecution is worse than slaughter. And fight not with them at the Sacred Mosque until they fight with you in it; so if they fight you (in it), slay them. Such is the recompense of the disbelievers. But if they desist, then surely Allah is Forgiving, Merciful. And fight them until there is no persecution, and religion is only for Allah. But if they desist, then there should be no hostility except against the oppressors" (Quran 2: 190-193).

It therefore is and has been incumbent upon all Muslims to jihad against oppression and has been from the beginning. It is not that Muslims are to jihad against non-Muslims, such would be ridiculous, the Prophet said concerning the *Mushriks*, "And thus their associate-gods have made fair-seeming to many polytheists the killing of their children, that they may cause them to perish and obscure for them their religion. And if Allah had pleased, they would not have done it, so leave them alone with that which they forge" (Quran 6: 137). "[L]eave them alone with that which they forge"! Hardly promoting jihad against all non-Muslims. But jihad was to be fought against oppression, all oppression, thus giving Islam a mission of permanent revolution right from the outset.

That said, we may now ask the question: how were the male chieftains, kings, Pharaohs, and Amirs able to hold back the female population, who at that time held all the secrets to knowledge, science, mysteries, and mysticism? Are White people able to do the same thing they did? And, if they are how can we stop them? These are all issues to be studied in social dynamics, which analyses the beginnings and endings of various social bodies. The study of social dynamics, just like the other methods of social mechanics, is based on formulaic computation and application. As mathematics works on the principle of formulae – once the correct formula has been discovered and applied any problem can be solved, but if an incorrect, inappropriate, or unfruitful formula is applied it will only lead to confusion, or worse, deception – so the branches of social mechanics are formulae for solving social problems.

Looking at social mechanics allows us to develop from an infinitude of non-linear events and ideas a quasi-linear progression from idea to event to new idea to new event. Thereby, in considering what we have been discussing so far, whereas with the patriarchy we may not know the exact cause of the male rise to power we are able to define a veritable concatenation with regard to White supremacy to devise theoretically the circumstances under which White people rose to power. If we consider the history of European and pan-European domination certain historical events become evident: Europe before the Renaissance was going through its Dark Ages, what the Renaissance did for Europe was to give to Europeans a unified identity and a common enemy in the Muslims. That is not to say there was no internal conflict, the Northern Renaissance is commonly known as the Reformation, in which many North European countries separated from the Catholic Church, instigating in some cases all-out war.

Nevertheless both Catholics and Protestants were united against the Muslims – whether the Muslim was Turk, Arab, Berber, Indian, or Moor – thus the climax of the Renaissance was *the enslavement of West Africans in 1441* and its justification in 1442 by Pope Eugene IV as anti-Muslim heroics. Popes Nicholas V, Sixtus IV, and Innocent VIII continued the anti-Muslim rhetoric instigating in Spain and Portugal a Reconquest, the culmination of which occurred in the early 1490s when the last of the African Moors were expelled from Spain, an event that was epilogued by Columbus' voyage to find the east of India. Indeed, the desire to find a back way to India was in itself nothing more than the result of his own anti-Muslim and anti-pagan proclivities: Columbus was a would-be Crusader, as were all the Conquistadors and the Reconquistadors; he set out to find a back way to the East coast of India as a spy for appropriate attack positions. Any form of slavery that was inflicted was justified by the Popes so long as it was against a non-Christian, and Luther had no argument with this kind of idea either.

From these humble positions Europe began its rise to domination, these are the events that began White supremacy. Prior to the Renaissance, the Reconquest, and the Trans-Atlantic Slave Trade; Africa and Asia were not going through Dark Ages like Europe was but were going through a period of immense enlightenment. Europe's enlightenment, which came over 200 years later, was based on lessons stolen and sometimes even plagiarised from Muslim intellectuals who wrote during Europe's Dark Ages. Europe was never able to compete with the Muslim world until they adopted Muslim systems, such as the Hindu-Arabic numerals, Muslim algebraic systems, Muslim economics, Muslim chemistry, Muslim geography, and Muslim astronomy.

Both Copernicus and Newton owed their knowledge of the motion of the planets to studies done originally by Islamic scholars like ibn Sina. But if Islam was the then dominant culture why was it surpassed by Europe during the 1700s and the European Enlightenment? And what has caused White people to maintain a form of supremacy ever since? Again, according to the Quran, "Allah never changes a favour which He has conferred upon a people until they change their own condition – and because Allah is Hearing, Knowing" (Quran 8: 53).

The European gained and maintained supremacy because the non-Europeans changed their condition; but that is only because White people demoralised and devalued them in a similar fashion to what was done to women. First, the so-called Negro, as Fanon said, for "the majority of white men … represents the sexual instinct (in its raw state). The Negro is the incarnation of a genital potency beyond all moralities and prohibitions." This stereotype was created by various White explorers and intellectuals due to the freedom and exhibitionism of the African subcultures they encountered. According to Fanon there exists to the White man, "Two realms: the intellectual and the sexual."

It was mainly by relegating the so-called Negro to the sexual realm, while, at the same time, devaluing sexuality, that White people were able to create the fiction of our racial inferiority; and though, as Fanon continued, "One can hear the glib remark: The Negro makes himself inferior … the truth is that he is made inferior." Yet, though such was true for the so-called Negro it was soon expanded to all Muslims as Said also noted, to the European, "An Oriental lives in the Orient, he lives a life of Oriental ease, in a state of Oriental despotism and sensuality, imbued with a feeling of Oriental fatalism". Effectively, the discourse of White superiority was always based on making the non-White an inferior player.

Effectively, Said presented a good argument with respect to Orientalism and its effect inside and outside the West: "My contention is that without examining Orientalism as a discourse one cannot possibly understand the enormously systematic discipline by which European culture was able to manage – and even produce – the Orient politically, sociologically, militarily, ideologically, scientifically, and imaginatively during the post-Enlightenment". Said also explicated how the transmutation of typology into stereotype took place in Europe with regard to the Oriental. Yet if this is the case for the Oriental it was even more so the case for the Black, as Fanon further articulated, "In Europe the Negro has one function: that of symbolizing the lower emotions, the baser inclinations, the dark side of the soul." "For the Negro is only biological. The Negroes are animals. They go about naked." Thus White supremacy is maintained first through devaluing sex, then by sexualising the other, whether it be women or Blacks. What is therefore needed is not the desexualisation of the other as such, but the revaluing of sexuality.

White supremacy has gone through a radical trans-formation since desegregation and decolonisation. Late modernity has produced three responses to its domination from the global population: secularism, Charismatism, and Islamism. Secularism (of the post-structuralists, postcolonialists, and postmodernists type) surrenders to three very obscure forms of nihilism: for the post-structuralist an anti-discursive nihilism, for the post-colonialist an anti-Western nihilism, and for the postmodernist an anti-science nihilism. All three represent three versions of neoliberalism and all these see truth in subversion and inversion (by the standards of what they are opposed to).

On the other hand, Charismatism (of both the Catholic and Protestant type) represents both an evangelical and eschatological response to late modernity. Both of these are neoconservative: the reactionary patriotism drawn from the merging of Christian morality and traditional values with political ideology and modern technology. However, what we have also been witnessing in our time is the evolution of this New Right (or neoconservative) response into the Alt-Rightism – whether they define themselves as such or not – of Christo-fascism. Recognising also that there already is an Alt-Left which leans closer to Stalinism I will say many of them still fall, whether implicitly or explicitly, under the banner of Christo-fascism, they just do not appreciate that. No, Stalinism, taken to the extreme is fascism, and Stalinism is nothing more than fascism with a working class face.

To be clear, none of these positions can be considered left-wing therefore we have moved into a new ideological permutation: the Right (whether New Right or Alt Right) has basically won for now, so be it. What we need to do at this point is find the synthesis between the neoconservative high conviction and the neoliberal low conviction. That synthesis is in anarcho-Islamism – or what *could* (and I emphasise could) be called neo-Islamism. It is the balance between high conviction leading to neoconservatism and low conviction leading to neoliberalism. It is a personal conviction leading to anarcho-Islamism. Such is what the godbody movement introduces.

True, though conviction can be inhibiting, anarchism must, by definition, be liberating. Anarchism delivers one from the curse of the law, while allowing them to fulfil the law being led by a new conviction – a conviction based on integrity. We must, however, also recognise that with us defining ourselves as anarcho-Islamists the equal and opposite reaction from the other side will be to become Christo-fascists. The truth is, however, that the Alt-Right is already basically just that: we are therefore the equal and opposite reaction to their aggression. So what is the true Alt-Left? Anarcho-Islamism. We represent that opposition to oppression that echoes throughout the ages. In this case, the Christo-fascists are, and will be, locked in an epic Armageddon with us for the destiny of humanity. For this cause, the real question remains: who will win?

Notwithstanding, the Quran also opens up for us new levels of racial interpretation against the White supremacy of the Christo-fascist type; as the Prophet said, "And of His signs is the creation of the heavens and the earth and the diversity of your tongues and colours. Surely there are signs in this for the learned" (Quran 30: 22). Almost with a sense of irony this argument is presented to the learned, who in modern times, that is, late modernity, seem to be in a controversy over the "race relations problematic." What the Prophet hereby showed was that the problem is not, and never was, racial categorisation, the racialisation of different human peoples; the problematic stems from racial stratification, the hierarchical arrangement of races into ascending layers.

Although most late modern social thinkers argue that the problematic lies in racial categorisation and the distinguishing of the biological, that is, physiological, differences between us, this Quranic statement showing that the different racial categories are a sign from Allah forces godbodyism to look deeper. Though such evidence as Quranic exegesis will not be enough for a scientific mind I will begin here to illuminate the historical distinction between modern and Islamic thinking. Shari'ati said on the subject, "Why is Islam, despite the lack of any capital investment or propaganda, so popular among African blacks? Because Islam is an ideology. What kind of an ideology? Whatever the black man's needs are. What are his needs? Freedom from discrimination and his longing for human equality" (Shari'ati 1981: 1932). Islam was able in its earlier years to encourage the brotherhood of all people and to embrace many races without disempowering or subjugating any for the sake of their racial differences, in spite of having a quasi-racial categorisation system, because they saw what we would call racial distinction as a sign from Allah. In fact, the racism many Arabs now possess comes primarily from Western education, whether directly or indirectly.

One of the central arguments presented by academics and social thinkers against racial categorisation is that the classical and scientific race theorists who initially attempted to categorise the races could never agree on the number of races. While such a reason is cute it is far from scientific and seems more lazy than thorough. Class is a categorisation system just as "socially constructed" as race, just as hierarchical as race, and just as controversial as race (most social scientists have not agreed on the number of classes or, indeed, the description of what constitutes a class, or what constitutes the existing classes of late modernity), yet the vast majority of social scientists and academics recognise the need for identifying class distinction and using such to explain social reality.

The Concatenation of Black Love

Here we see that it is not the physical conditions of the person that places them in subjugation, but the mental, that is, the psychological reasonings of the person that subjugates them. In this line of thought the Quran says, "And when We said to the angels: Be submissive to Adam, they submitted except Iblis; he refused. We said: O Adam, this is an enemy to thee and to thy wife; so let him not drive you both out of the garden [Jannah] so that thou art unhappy. Surely it is granted to thee therein that thou art not hungry, nor naked, And that thou art not thirsty therein, nor exposed to the sun's heat. But the devil made an evil suggestion to him; he said: O Adam, shall I lead thee to the tree of immortality and a kingdom which decays not? So they both ate of it, then their evil inclinations became manifest to them" (Quran 20: 116-121). See, the truth is, only by letting go and losing ourselves in libido can we find a way to re-enter Jannah to be with Allah.

It is written, again, "Surely Allah will make those who believe and do good deeds enter Gardens [Jannah] wherein flow rivers – they are adorned therein with bracelets of gold and (with) pearls. And their garments therein are of silk. And they are guided to pure words, and they are guided to the path of the Praised One" (Quran 22: 23). Thus Jannah is opened to those that find libido and lose themselves to its guidance. Indeed, this losing of self to libido is and must be first expressed in love of self, but ultimately, and with maturity, we find it includes a letting go of self. Still, the letting go of self being the highest manifestation of a self-sacrificing yet unquenchable love, is that libidinal love that comes from a combination of Pathos (which is itself a combination of agape and empathy) and Eros (which is based primarily on sensuality), a libidinal love that can only be respected when the truth of monism is appreciated. In these instances suffering comes from the flesh and a desire to preserve the flesh and not from imperfection or from modern injustices.

In their own desire to show love to other groups, the Black Panthers, known usually as a militant and aggressively masculine group, began to voice and advocate for what, in today's manosphere, is considered anathema: women and gays "Oh my!" Newton said back in the 1970s, way before it became popular, "[W]e say that we recognize the women's right to be free. … And I know through reading and through my life experience, my observations, that homosexuals are not given freedom and liberty by anyone in the society. Maybe they might be the most oppressed people in the society." High praise from a legend in the Black Power movement, and high shame to those in the Black manosphere who themselves also perpetuate the marginalisation of these groups.

The level of sensitivity and empathy it took for Newton, who himself was not a homosexual, to stand up for and with the LGBTQIA community during the 1970s, when homophobia was still very strong, particularly in the Black community, was awesome. Due to the deafness of most Black militants to the realities of the LGBTQIA community I have to grudgingly say that I myself am not gay, bi, or trans, nor have I ever been. Also that one does not need to be a part of the LGBTQIA community to sympathise with their fight against the same enemy we all have of the Victorian monogamous patriarchal standard of masculinity. Effectively, as Ratele noted, "Sexual disgust, hatred and stigma are the end products generated by patriarchal heterosexual structures, integral to the very constitution of patriarchy and heterosexuality. Conversely, the sexual guilt or shame we experience when men feel sexually stirred up by other men is thus also an effect of the prevailing structures."

Such cases of hegemonic masculinity being weaponised against Black men and boys obviously also exists within the camp of both heterosexual and hypersexual men. In this instance, as stated by Douglas, "Black men were regarded, like their female counterparts, as highly sexualized, passionate beings. They were considered lewd, lascivious, and also quite sexually proficient. Black male sexual prowess has become almost legend in the stereotypic logic of White culture. The idea that Black men possess an unusually large penis has only reinforced notions of their sexual aggressiveness and mastery." But such pressure is not the only problematic related to certain myths of Black masculinity. According to Sheller, "Popular figures of African masculinity and military prowess [also] served a significant function in materially achieving and symbolically marking the transition from slavery to freedom in many parts of the Americas. [And v]iolence anointed manhood in many post-slavery contexts but especially in Haiti, where freedom was won by force of arms."

The situation is even more complex still as, if we consider also the current standard in the hood, and especially with regard to young Black women, most people in the hood have not only adopted the Victorian monogamous patriarchal standard with regard to masculinity – that a man's central duty is to be a provider and a protector to women and children, particularly his own wife and children – but they use judgmental and punitive measures to enforce it on all the boys that grow up in the hood. This Victorian model of hegemonic masculinity may not be the only form of toxic masculinity but it is definitely the most dominant and pervasive. Yet such an image or identity effectively falls apart when a woman can provide for herself and/or her family without the need of a male figure in her life. This has been the first blow to hegemonic masculinity, particularly in the Black community, where, though she is very likely to get cheated on wages, a Black woman is far more likely to get a job on the job-market than a Black man. Plus, far more likely to have a college or university degree.

These leave Black men with one means of asserting their manhood: protection, or the lack thereof. Here we see many women beginning to arm themselves, on the one hand, and learn unarmed martial arts, on the other. All this has effectively rendered the Black man virtually irrelevant by the Victorian standard of masculinity, leaving the Black manosphere with nothing to do but moan and complain that Black women hate Black men. Obviously, such an assumption is bogus as most Black women would much rather have a Black husband or boyfriend than any other. Still, his own inadequacies cause him to doubt her sincerity. It is hard to argue with them either on this point, as, though Black women generally tend to praise and honour Black men and speak on our strength, power, and endurance against racism and oppression; on an individual or personal level those same Black women will be, and have definitely been, approached by Black men that get shot down instantly. These Black men know in their heart of hearts that they were only rejected because they did not meet the typical standard of a "high value" Black man.

Yet, as the Quran also teaches us they were themselves created for us: "And of His signs is this, that He created you from dust, then lo! you are mortals (who) scatter. And of His signs is this, that He created mates for you from yourselves that you might find quiet of mind in them, and He put between you love and compassion. Surely there are signs in this for a people who reflect" (Quran 30: 20, 21). Moreover, this love and compassion were never meant to simply be taken as sterile concepts but active realities within human affairs even as they were with the first couple. It is said in both the Bible and the Quran that Adam and Eve dwelt in Paradise before the fall, and that all their godly children will one day return to Paradise having completed their worldly travels.

Still, this Paradise, coming from the Hebrew word Eden and the Arabic word Edin is a lot more beautiful than most Christian interpretations have appreciated. Accordingly, the word Eden in Hebraic means voluptuous, luxuriant, and given to pleasures. Furthermore, its Hebraic root Adan means: ecstatic and pleasant. Even its feminine *Ednah* in its original Hebraic means ecstasy, voluptuousness, and pleasure; yet here it is in the *erotic* sense of the words. Basically, what can be seen by a true definition of the word Paradise, in its Hebraic and Arabic meanings is that it is more a place of delights, both sensual and spiritual, and all these are promised to the righteous children of Adam.

Consequently, though it could now be said that we Black people hold a special place being the authentic children of Adam, in order to enter this Paradise we and all humanity will one day have to give an account of what we have done with the good Allah has given us, as it is said, "And surely We have honoured the children of Adam, and We carry them in the land and the sea, and We provide them with good things, and We have made them to excel highly most of those whom We have created. On the day when We shall call every people with their leader: then whoever is given his book in his right hand, these will read their book; and they will not be dealt with a whit unjustly." "So wait patiently for the judgment of thy Lord, and obey not a sinner or an ungrateful one among them. And glorify [*dhikr*] the name of thy Lord morning and evening" (Quran 17: 70, 71; 76: 24, 25).

So now, who is to blame for the current Incel paradox in the Black community? The Black females for having high standards? The Black males for not being ambitious enough? The Victorian monogamous patriarchal standard of hegemonic masculinity for creating a goal unreachable for most men? Or White society for promoting and trying to enforce this standard on other races? Whatever choice you choose, and all of them are worthy of note, it does nothing to improve Black love or fix Black love, which, we have to admit at this point, is broken. We, in the Black community, therefore, more than ever, need a new standard of masculinity; and the godbody, to a high degree, has provided just that.

In the Nation of Gods and Earths a Black man, at least to a certain degree, is judged more on his level of knowledge (science) than his level of income. Also, as many females within the godbody, though not all admittedly, at least currently, are able to protect themselves through armed and unarmed violence; it is the Black God's integrity above all else, so long as he has integrity, that elevates his position. Do not get it twisted though, outside the godbody movement most Black women still hold to the Victorian monogamous patriarchal standard of hegemonic masculinity. It is only a few Black sisters scattered here and there that actually value intelligence and integrity. These, however, are usually Black Goddesses, Afrocentric Queens, conscious or womanist sisters, or ride-or-die thugettes. Like the proverbial needle in the haystack to most Black men outside their communities, these Black women are for the most part out of their reach so they end up turning to a community where they feel accepted as Black men.

I have not written all this to justify the overt misogynoirism of the Black manosphere, nor to justify Black male violence on, or rape of, Black women, and definitely not to blame Black women for all the current problems in and with Black love. I have written it to show that the issue of Black love is a lot more complex than Black men needing to step up or Black women secretly hating Black men while praising them with their mouths. Again, the cure for the so-called death of Black love is to define a new standard of Black masculinity and Black femininity.

Here the Horu construct and Hethor construct represent the perfect preliminary to the actual accomplishment of Ausar or Auset consciousness. Horu has hypermartiality, hyperintegrity, and hyperintelligence; while Hethor has hypersexuality, hyperspirituality, and also hyperintelligence. These, of all things, should be the Black standard, not money, fame, power, innocence, decency, modesty, or "status." Indeed, most of the slaves and colonised had none of these symbols of Victorian masculinity or femininity, yet they still loved each other and had loving families and communities. Black love worked during those times because nobody accepted the White system as workable for Blacks even if nowadays it seems we do.

To finalise this point: the Black God shows his godhood through martiality, integrity, and intelligence (again, science); these are all internal qualities that any man can develop easy without trusting the unreliable market (whether job-market, product market, brand market, idea market, corporate market, stock market, or any direct response or content marketers), to help us to become rich and thereby "valuable." The same with the Black Goddess, she demonstrates her divinity through her sexuality, spirituality, and intelligence, which, again, are all internal qualities all Black women possess but can refine and develop; as against the current White standard of "decency" or "modesty." As for the Black man's martiality and the Black woman's sexuality, it is undeniable that these internal drives also have external manifestations. Yet, the tough (strong) Black man and the hot (beautiful) Black woman are by the definition of the beholder: as in most cases.

The Horu construct of the ancient Egyptian king and the modern Black child is one which should manifest his journey towards divinity. When the Horu child is raised by an Auset he is on the right path. She will give him his rituals and spirituality from early youth. The lessons he learns in early youth he will not forget when he gets older. When he learns to cleanse the body with water and lotions, and when he learns to treasure his body as that of a holy God that is a start to him viewing the female body as that of a holy temple for him to enter into.

The living Pharaohs of ancient Kemet (ancient Egypt) were all considered to be Horu in the flesh; thus they were considered the embodiment of Black majesty. And as Horu conquered Setekh (the satanic force) in the story, so the Pharaoh conquered the forces of injustice and oppression in the world. He was the personification of the warrior, even as the Black man currently is today. However, when the king died he would travel to the stars to be one with Ausar. Thus the dead king became Ausar, the force that helped and protected the living king. Considering these realities, perhaps the best way to explain all the beauties and glories of the Black family is to define them from the perspective not of a socialising, but of an organising and a purifying.

The Black Horu son and Hethor daughter should be taught this pure and clean lifestyle along with sexuality so as to understand their sexuality from a young age for the purpose of heightening their sensuality and understanding of their erotogenous zones. That is not to say that they should be allowed to do adult things, like start having sex or stop wearing underwear: they should merely be taught about sex to know their bodies more and how to control their baser, more instinctual sensations better. Learning control over their sexual energies from a young age would give them a closer connection to the deity by the time they reach adolescence so that they would be able to become true Ausars and Ausets in adulthood.

In actual fact, the Nilotic Black boy who was raised as a Horu developed an interconnection to the ancient Pharaohs of Kush and Kemet, seeing self as a divine manifestation. And, as the Messiah himself represented a Horu in his own time and the living Pharaohs represented a Horu in their own time, even so Ausar represented the Allah of the Asarian apocalypse, being the personification of libido and of the dead ancestors of the Black family. Where the Messiah reigns in the heart the person must, like the Messiah, fight against all manifestations of injustice and unrighteousness. By struggling for freedom, justice, and equality the Messiah proved himself to be a true Horu, but by hanging from a tree he proved himself to be a true Ausar. Yet it is knowledge that ultimately allowed him to be one with all the dead Pharaohs of history, the dead Black kings and queens, and all the righteous dead ancestors of the Black family; who also see and have seen all that has been going on in the world at the hands of the Western powers.

Adam and Black Excellence

What we can ultimately understand is that knowledge brought forth Adam's greatest exaltation and knowledge brought forth his greatest failure, Allah trusted Adam with knowledge of self and thereby made him his *Khalifah* but Adam, through trick knowledge, fell, together with his wifey, from all that grace and abundance, having been corrupted by the prideful Iblis. And so "he caused them to fall by deceit. So when they had tasted of the tree, their shame became manifest to them, and they both began to cover themselves with the leaves of the garden [Jannah]. And their Lord called to them: Did I not forbid you that tree, and say to you that the devil is surely your open enemy? They said: Our Lord, we have wronged ourselves; and if Thou forgive us not, and have (not) mercy on us, we shall certainly be of the losers" (Quran 7: 22, 23).

Notice that in the Quran they did not blame Allah, saying, "You made us like this," "You made our circumstances like this," or "You made the world like this." Nor did they say, "It is not our fault for, 'His is whosoever is in the heavens and the earth. All are obedient to Him' (Quran 30: 26) therefore we are not to blame." Neither did Adam blame the woman, saying, "It was 'The woman whom thou gavest to be with me' (Genesis 3: 12) that caused me to fall." Instead they were wise enough to seek mercy after their fall; and as they sought mercy, even so they received mercy, "Then Adam received (revealed) word from his Lord, and He turned to him (mercifully). Surely He is Oft-returning (to mercy), the Merciful. We said: Go forth from this (state) all. Surely there will come to you a guidance from Me, then whoever follows My guidance, no fear shall come upon them, nor shall they grieve" (Quran 2: 37, 38). Blame and irresponsibility pepper the biblical story of Adam and Eve but not the Quranic. Furthermore, guidance is promised to those who accept Allah's teachings.

When knowledge comes from Allah it completes us just as it completed Adam, but when we forget the teachings taught us by Allah we become vulnerable to trick knowledge; again just like Adam, "Supremely exalted then is Allah, the King, the Truth. And make not haste with the Qur'an before its revelation is made complete to thee, and say: My Lord, increase me in knowledge. And certainly We gave a commandment to Adam before, but he forgot; and We found in him no resolve" (Quran 20: 114, 115). Thus Adam's fall was more an issue of forgetting the knowledge he gained from Allah's teaching, and his trusting in the *tricknology* he gained from his enemy, than of his eating a fruit in the eternal Jannah.

Indeed, Iblis has always been an enemy of Adam, as it was written, "He said: O Iblis, what is the reason that thou art not with those who make obeisance? He said: I am not going to make obeisance to a mortal, whom Thou hast created of sounding clay, of black mud fashioned into shape." Again, when asked the reason he would not make obeisance to Adam Iblis did not say, "And whoever is in the heavens and the earth makes obeisance to Allah only" (Quran 15: 32). The Quran says of Allah, "He said: What hindered thee that thou didst not submit when I commanded thee? He said: I am better than he; Thou hast created me of fire, while him Thou didst create of dust" (Quran 33; 13: 15; 7: 12). Herein, the reason for the fall of Iblis, and of humanity, was racism. Iblis felt superior to Adam and so became a sworn enemy of Adam.

Furthermore, the Prophet also recognised a preordained element to this enmity, saying, "The devil threatens you with poverty and enjoins you to be [weary], and Allah promises you forgiveness from Himself and abundance. And Allah is Ample-giving, Knowing." Indeed, "when He gave them out of His grace, they became [weary] of it and they turned away and they are averse." But this weakness of Adam's was also of preordained origin, "Allah desires to make light your burdens, and man is created weak. O you who believe, devour not your property among yourselves by illegal methods except that it be trading by your mutual consent" (Quran 2: 268; 9: 76; 4: 28, 29).

Moreover, the poverty of humanity is effected not by the lack of production, or even the lack of the will to trade, but by the lack of consumption, when people are unable to afford to trade. Even in our day, as Dr. King also understood, "We have come to the point where we must make the nonproducer a consumer or we will find ourselves drowning in a sea of consumer goods. We have so energetically mastered production that we now must give attention to distribution. Though there have been increases in purchasing power, they have lagged behind increases in production." Interestingly, we Black people seem to regularly be the producers, workers, or consumers; never or rarely the owners. Why is that? Such owners are entrepreneurs, capitalists, or petty capitalists, that is, Black capitalists.

Notwithstanding, as Black Panther cofounder Bobby Seale explained, "we will not fight capitalism with black capitalism; we will not fight imperialism with black imperialism; [and] we will not fight racism with black racism". "For what is a man profited, if he shall gain the whole world, and lose his own soul? or what shall a man give in exchange for his soul?" (Matthew 16: 26). Herein lies the problem with the myth of Black excellence. While seeming to be a great successor to Black Power, Black excellence: the recognition in the Black community of the values of Black capitalism and Black imperialism (whether with corporate empires or street empires), has dangerously corrupted the Black American community, who, for a time, were considered the strategically placed vanguard of the global revolution.

Essentially, if we were to look, with a serious eye, at the three biggest Black movements to have transpired since the rise of the Obamas we would start to understand something very interesting. These movements were: Black excellence, Black girl magic, and Black Lives Matter, respectively; and as wonderful and necessary as they may have been, and in some cases still are, they did not address the deep issues at the heart of the Black struggle. Issues that could ultimately change and affect the Black condition in America. This has been the central problem with the eight-yearlong Obama administration, as wonderful as it was to see a Black family in the White House, one that became aspirations/goals for so many Black bourgeoisies; they actually, in the substantial sense, accomplished very little on the ground for Black Americans. In fact, if we were to take an honest look at America today I think we would find that the Obama victories may have in fact negatively impacted race relations in America.

Consequently, one of the biggest problems with the current generation – I know, I have basically become the old man yelling at clouds – is most Gen Zers grew up during the Obama administration and under the influence of the

Black American elite. Effectively, Black Americans had moved from dreams of Black power to dreams of Black excellence; and thus, the exemplary Negro, the House Negro, became goals or became aspirations. He looked better, dressed better, acted cooler, and was more accepted and beloved by the White slavemaster class than any of us field slaves could ever have hoped to be. They grew up, not with images of Black men and women with guns and leather jackets, nor of Black men and women wearing traditional African clothing and jewellery. "That's old shit!" so they say. No, they grew up with images of corporate suits; the rise of the benevolent Black billionaire; and a successful Black monogamous patriarchal family in the White House. They therefore received all the proof they needed that the system can and does work, even for us. But does it though?

First, as YouTube influencer lil' bill pointed out on his channel, in order to be a Black capitalist one must be a capitalist of Black skin colour. Well, in order to be a *good* capitalist, of whatever colour, one must start, build, and own a successful business. Herein lies the rub. If a business does not have at least one other person, working at a decent wage, who is employed by the owner, it will in all likelihood fail, or struggle, until it eventually fails. But such a statement further implies a second rub: most Black businesses are unable to hire a single employee outside of the owner due to lack of start-up funding or extra resources, and so, in most cases, are or become, unable to generate any more than $30,000 in annual revenue.

The obvious solution the average Black liberal or entrepreneurial dreamer will throw at this difficulty is to encourage the people to "Buy Black." The problem with this solution, however, is that most non-White businesses, and particularly "Black-owned" businesses, face the struggle of not being valued as much as White businesses in most cases, especially when in start-up mode. On top of that, due to lack of the funding capacity that most White businesses take for granted, whether from banks, angel investors, or venture funding (which includes the slick online crowd support funding) lack the means to make it passed the pivotal phase of ignorance, experimentation, and trial and error. Thus they rarely make it out of the realm of pure survival and into the realm of true profit-making. Not to mention most of the so-called spending power of the Black world goes toward survival, including paying debts and bills; not toward generating any real wealth or "giving back" to the community.

At the same time, the perceptive Black and non-White people know that Black excellence, as well as aspiring to such heights, is, and will always be, an unreachable dream for the average Black/non-White person. But what is their answer? "Don't be average." Okay, so here I was putting out mediocre bullshit for nothing! What I really should have been doing was following that age old mantra of Black excellence: work twice as hard to receive half as much pay and credit as White people(!). Indeed, one group of capitalists also say to work hard, go the extra mile, put in extra time, prepare extra well for all eventualities, and soon your entrepreneurial venture will succeed. Then another group of capitalists instead say: no, those guys that work hard and trust in grind and hustle are all idiots. You need to leverage the latest technology, leverage funding, leverage your employees (the Team), and leverage any other asset or resource you can get your hands on; then you will succeed. The truth is, neither group knows what the hell they are talking about.

Success, in a capitalistic system, comes about only, only, by the chaotic, erratic, and sporadic whims of the invisible hand as it guides the market. Neither hard work, grind, and preparation; nor leverage, technology, and a sophisticated team can generate success. Nothing can. Nothing … Maybe prayer(?). Literally, the Prophet himself said, "… Surely Allah changes not the condition of a people, until they change their own condition. And when Allah intends evil to a people, there is no averting it, and besides Him they have no protector" (Quran 13: 11).

Whenever a business is starting there will always be mistakes in the beginning. This is why start-up funding is so vital. While a business is going through its teething phase it needs something to keep it alive. Without that respirator the business will die immediately. Most entrepreneur success stories usually fail to explain, or at least they under-explain, the significance of start-up capital. Whether from outside existing employment, bank loans, angel investment, or giving away equity, start-ups, all start-ups, *will* fail without capital to keep them alive. Period. The reason most businesses started by celebrities usually, though not always, succeed is because they usually have enough capital to invest in their business to get them passed that awkward start-up phase.

Thus the secret to capitalistic success is not work hard, grind, and hustle; nor becoming an early adopter of some disruptive new technology. The secret to capitalistic success to a degree is having the funding to keep going until reaching breakthrough (the law of compounding/repetition theory). However, even this in many cases does not work and business owners hold on too long to a product, idea, or venture that just will not sell. For this cause, true success in the capitalistic system, for Black, White, or anybody is pure hope in market forces – the most unreliable entities in the universe. Thereby, Black entrepreneurs, guided by the myth of Black excellence and a die hard, iron willed, dogged determination continue on because, "Quitters never win!" Try saying that one to a recovering alcoholic.

So then, if Black capitalism is not the key to the progress of the Black community, what economic system should be? Black syndicalism. Black syndicalism is based on the adoption of trades councils (TCs). These should be set up together with co-operatives to guarantee that working people have their say about the conditions of their work and should co-ordinate with distribution councils (DCs) on what will be needed and desired from them in a given month. The DCs, on the other hand, should receive all consumption and distribution requests from the local, district, regional, and national distribution councils every month and discuss shopping trends. They should also have an annual meeting to receive annual consumption and distribution requests for production and allocation analysis.

This would effectively be the best way to organise and co-ordinate all domestic labour and distribution practices within the Black thearchist movement. At current capitalism works on a system of market domination; syndicalism, on the other hand, would work on a system of syndicate domination. Effectively, the syndicate or TC, can be a parliament (discussion ground) or a federation (organisation ground), yet while I recognise that organisation is important and that talk without action is useless, we need to set our priorities straight. Organisation without a proper foundation or discussion process is like putting up a building without drawing up and perfecting the blueprint. Herein the suggestion is being made that the central organ for the TCs be parliamentary.

True, Bor and Bor did say, "For Cole, TCs [already] constituted local *trade union parliaments* fostering the spirit of trade union solidarity" (Bor & Bor 2024: xxxvii), we must not lose sight of this truism to chase ideological uncertainties. Though, also, for the most part, "Syndicalists, including Tom Mann and Jack Tanner … envisaged [TCs] as the embryonic organisation of a new system of workers self-organisation" (Bor & Bor 2024: 37), that did not diminish their understanding that these bodies had to function through discussion and debate, even if Mann and Tanner both supported the idea of a National Federation of Trades Councils (NFTC).

The parliamentary alternative to the NFTC in England was the Trades Councils Joint Consultative Committee (TCJCC). Again, TCs were very capable of centralising but for the most part remained decentralised, and organised mainly at local levels. They collaborated and corresponded with the TUC (Trade Union Congress) but were separate from their authority. That said, "Since its inception in 1920, the [British Communist Party] had an ambition – to democratise the TUC as a Parliament of Labour, including TC representatives" (Bor & Bor 2024: 42). Here, they also shared "a vision of *comprehensive TCs*, political, industrial and co-operative bodies with an information bureau on landlords, capitalists, shopkeepers and 'blacklegs' (strike-breakers). These visionary functions … included training workers in the management of local affairs" (Bor & Bor 2024: 43). Their vision of trades councils were essentially to be like mini-governments of workers organised for the progression of the people.

This is fundamentally different from capitalism, which is run by the chaotic market and wage system. Any intelligent person, however, should know that a business plan followed is more likely to achieve success than just leaving things to the market, and that an economic plan followed is more likely to achieve success than trusting in some mysterious forces to *correct* all instabilities. Trusting in TCs to govern decision-making is thereby far more reliable than trusting in market forces to correct social equities with business failures, job-losses, and economic downturns. Indeed, a decentralised planned economy should be the aim of all genuinely progressive movements; especially for the purpose of building and maintaining communicational, educational, psychological, ideological, sociological, industrial, and commercial institutions within their neighbourhood and community.

Furthermore, we must be sure that the TCs and DCs are able to remunerate their members accordingly for services rendered, particularly for coming to regular meetings. For example, I say there should be no underwear worn by any of our members ever. In remunerating this behaviour members will have to first start to shower after every time they take a shit, and then lotion and cologne/perfume their privates. The remuneration will be based on the fact that those who smell the best among us will clearly be those not wearing underwear and wearing cologne/perfume on their privates. The actual remuneration itself will be credibility in the councils, which I believe should be parliaments. Indeed, instead of the old capitalist mantra of, "If you don't work you don't eat," we need to climatise ourselves to the syndicalist mantra of, "If you do well you make a name for yourself."

Effectively, we should set up think tanks, co-operatives, martial education and training, sexual education and training, community support industries (including food banks, clothing banks, commercial banks, financial banks, investment banks, medical support, communal nursing and midwifery, communal childraising, communal protection, and communal sanitation and homemaking services), production industries (including publishing, computing, engineering, construction, architecture, carpentry, herding, agriculture, biodiversity, clean energy, and clean tech developing), and distribution industries (including logistics, robotics, warehousing, planning, retailing, promoting, allocating, shipping, trucking, and couriering) all effectively having their own councils and giving us credibility as a Nation. With all these bodies and institutions thus put in place the chaotic malaise existing in many ghettos today as a result of the uneven financial and territorial development caused by the market would essentially be ended.

Moreover, all the parliaments should aim to be organised so as to have only between 3-100 members each. That is, they should have no more than a hundred members total in each meeting. The moment a meeting gets more than a hundred members they should then begin the process of splitting and separating, deciding from that time what territorial boundaries they will set for each branch – while still remaining under the umbrella of the godbody movement – wherein is the unity of the entire movement. Basically, we should never host massive parliaments like the Christians host megachurches. Our goal should be efficiency not prestige. Prestige will come, but not from the size of our meetings, rather from the size of our movement.

The truth is, however, that godbodyism, as a movement, is not a utopian ideal painting a picture of a Paradise or a better world or system. We already have our Paradise, we just seek to have the right to narrate, legitimate, represent, and reproduce our Paradise without the fear of government persecution, or public ostracism, stigmatisation, or humiliation for doing so. In this, we do not seek to enter into a battle with the government: there are many animal kingdoms within nature that are able to peacefully coexist without any substantial disturbances. We simply seek and desire the right to an interdependent living: that is, to narrate and perform our culture our way without governmental or bourgeois attempts at intimidation or subordination of us. For this we are, and must remain, willing to fight to the death, even with the use of violence, to achieve this right. In this, our bravery will be demonstrated by our unwillingness to bow down to government coercions or bourgeois distortions, and by our unwillingness to hypocritically try to turn our Black divines into Black bourgeoisies.

The Making of a Ghetto Ideology

The apostle John reassures us in our ideological progression, saying: "I write unto you, little children, because your sins are forgiven you for his name's sake. I write unto you, fathers, because ye have known him that is from the beginning. I write unto you, young men, because you have overcome the wicked one" (1John 2: 12, 13). Even Antonio Gramsci, an Italian political prisoner during Mussolini's Fascist dictatorship, also explained this kind of social superstructure for political social bodies:

1. The principle element, which is the nerve centre. In here you have the mind of the party, body, or organisation. They themselves are a group of individuals who agree on an outcome and dictate their idea to others. As the nerve centre this group represents the most important element within the body. Whether by their passion and charisma or their devotion and discipline, these individuals will be the party or organisation leaders.

2. The intermediate element, which are those who follow the nerve centre. These take the ideas from the leading members and transmit them to the ordinary, non-organisational members. They are the

go-betweens as every big party and organised body needs representatives to go-between the central views of the principle element and the broader masses of the body.

3. The mass element, which are those who follow the intermediaries. The mass element are what could be called the rank-and-file. They give the party or organised body its size and strength as well as its connection to the real world of the non-affiliated mass. Though a group can exist and function without them it will not last too long nor will it remain too powerful. These, again, represent the normal everyday people who routinise the ideas and understandings transmitted to them by the intermediate element and bring them into a social context.

Any revolutionary movement in the truest sense of the word would need a unified and organised leadership committee in order to function in a unified and progressive way. In the case of the godbody the leadership is clearly the captains, the intermediaries would be the lieutenants, and the mass element would be the soldiers. But the leaders must also be guided by the goals and principles of the Five Percent Nation and by a desire to fulfil its ultimate destiny. This also means being guided by our values and ethics until they have become standardised within our hearts. The Black thearchy could be the ideology of the godbody – we have only taken the lessons of the godbody to the next level. The Black thearchy itself is a progressive movement from the godbody, to organise our movement into a social programme that incorporates the general ideas and practices of the godbody and makes them applicable to society at large, particularly the Black community.

At the same time, our message of justice and ethics must not be compromised for the sake of appeasing White or bourgeois critics, or even White or bourgeois scholars seeking to speak for us. In order to prevent this from happening we godbodies must become more dogmatic with regard to our lessons and teachings. Let me be clear though: I do not mean here the introduction of religious dogmas. What I mean is to set a demarcation point beyond which one either comes dangerously closing to leaving our system, or they compromise dramatically our self-conception and self-determination. While I recognise that dogma does have an air of religiosity about it, the truth is still the truth and to be dogmatic with the truth is to be free from the lie, whatever shape the lie comes in.

As German Marxist reformer Ferdinand Lassalle once said: "a party's weakness is its diffuseness and the blurring of clear demarcations; a party becomes stronger by purging itself" (Lasselle 1852; quoted in Lenin 2020: 43). We must therefore decide on what doctrine is formal godbody and what doctrine will not fly. This is the hope of Black thearchism: to elevate the godbody movement into a formalised structure that is both credible and creditable; so that, even if we do unify with those who have misled the Black community to the point of denying their own culture and history, we will not be corrupted by them, and we will have several strong points on which we stand. Effectively, as the old aphorism says, "If you will stand for nothing you will fall for anything."

While it may be true that godbodyism as it stands today already practices a high level of dogmatic discipline, we still currently do not have within our movement a fully and universally accepted interpretation or system that we all acknowledge and respect. For a start, we do not even have a current social or cultural signifier that distinguishes us from every other movement. To be sure, within the Fruit of Islam they have their suit and bow tie, within Christianity they have their crosses, within the super-gangs they have their bandana and colours, within the Rastafari they have their Dreadlocks, and with the Afrocentrics they have their traditional African clothing. We may say we ourselves have the crown and head-covering, but the truth is, these do not distinguish us as a movement. They were appropriated from Islam, therefore those who see us with our crown (*kufi*) or head-covering (usually a head-wrap) do not recognise us as a God or Goddess but instead see us as either a Muslim or an Afrocentric.

We need a distinguishing signifier, one that is ours and ours alone, not just for the purpose of identification but also for the purpose of branding. It is for this reason that I suggest as the first and fundamental practice of our movement the adopting by all members, male and female, young and old, of the wearing of the universal flag everywhere and at all times. To explain what I mean a little deeper: I do not mean the wearing of the universal flag as a tattoo or chain everywhere but the wearing of an actual universal flag bandana. Still, admittedly, even this move is not distinguished as such.

However, we can distinguish ourselves by how we wear the universal flag. Herein, the suggestion is that a rule be made for all godbodies, from the time we become newborns, that we tie the bandana of the universal flag around our left bicep and only around our left bicep. That means: it is never to be worn anywhere on the body of a God or Goddess but on the left bicep, not even on the left hand, shoulder, or forearm. This one practice will distinguish us as a movement and allow those in all the other Black movements to see that we are becoming more structured and more systematised. Again, all professional movements have a uniform or mark of distinction. As the universal flag is already of high value within our movement we should therefore express that value by wearing it everywhere. This distinguishing mark and the enforcement of strict discipline with regards to wearing it everywhere, will, however, only be a preliminary step.

It should be clear to those who currently follow our tradition that us not having a clearly defined stance on issues we profess to be important to us is also inexcusable. We must therefore all have a substantive knowledge and understanding of our overall vision, and also on the objectives by which we plan to achieve our vision. Following Jim Collins and Jerry I. Porras: in order to find our vision and to find the objectives by which we plan to achieve our vision we must, first, answer three initial questions, then, answer three further questions. First, (i) what are our core and our adjacent values, (ii) what is our core purpose, and (iii) what is our BHAG as a movement. Then, (i) what is the Hedgehog Concept that will best explain our responsibilities as a movement, (ii) what is the flywheel we will have to turn to fulfil our responsibilities as a movement, and (iii) what is the 20 Mile March we will have to reach with maximum consistency to fulfil our responsibilities as a movement. While these may be figured out on an individual basis they must also be understood on a social body-wide basis too.

Based on the Collins and Porras ideas concerning various visionary companies that were built to last we can see that having a vision is fundamental to a company's stability and survival (Collins & Porras 2005). Using the Collins and Porras definition of vision: a vision is generally based on a business, corporation, or organisation finding its own core values, core purpose, and a BHAG to commit itself to. The same is true for a social movement/social enterprise; and as godbodyism is itself a social movement/social enterprise, we will therefore need, first and foremost, to find, know, and understand what Hofstede called our "deeply rooted values: things that are preferred by or desirable to the group." Yet, in order to find this we must before that define what a value actually is. According to Erdman, "American anthropologist Clyde Kluckholhn's concept of [a value], described [it] as 'a *conception* ... of the desirable which influences the selection from available modes, means and ends of actions.' In other words, values are thoughts and actions that are important to individuals within a society and are reinforced over time to define the group" (Erdman 2017: 36, 22; emphasis mine).

Based on the use of this kind of terminology we can see that values themselves are basically specific kinds of conceptions or concepts that we have given meaning to. Hereby, if we wish to find, know, and understand our values, we must start by finding and understanding what our core, adjacent, and peripheral concepts are, within their own ideological morphologies (Freeden 2013). If we now consider the genuine morphology of our social movement/ social enterprise then we can see how the core concepts of our movement should be the key values contained in the Black DREADS acronym: Black divinity, Black revolutionism, Black eroticism, Black astralism, Black demodernisation, and Black syndicalism.

At the same time, we should maintain as our adjacent concepts the key values of the LEADERSHIP acronym: L-look, listen and learn. E-evolve with education. A-accelerate with action. D-do your duty and fulfil your obligations as a civilized person. E-everything should be done with equality. R-respond with results and respect. S-set superior standards and provide selfless-service. H-have honest and open communication. I-input with intelligence and integrity. P-personal courage, positive attitude, and purpose. The reason I call these adjacent concepts and not core concepts is because they are more aspirational than already actively practiced. The core concepts are actually, for the most part, actively practiced within the current godbody culture. Finally, our peripheral concepts can be whatever the Gods and Goddesses consider to be important in the moment such as national consciousness and community control.

That said, with every movement there is also always decided their core purpose: something they believe worth fighting for, something they believe worth dying for, something that they are willing to spend their entire lives seeking to bring into the world. Based on our 120 lessons I think our core purpose should remain: to build a world of love, peace, and happiness. This must stay our Polaris and our true north, and, therefore, our overall purpose as a movement. A purpose that may not be fulfilled in the lifetime of many of those alive today, but that we will keep fighting for for another hundred, or even ten-thousand years. This is our dream, a dream that we will keep aspiring towards regardless of the oppositions and challenges that may arise to prevent its fulfilment. The difference between a purpose and a goal is that a goal may be fulfilled in our lifetime but a purpose may take hundreds or even thousands of years to be fulfilled. A world of love, peace, and happiness is a godbody dream worth fighting for and gives direction to our currently directionless movement.

However, we godbodies currently do not even have a universal goal that we all aspire towards. It is here, therefore, that I would like to introduce to us godbodies the concept of the BHAG (Big Hairy Audacious Goal) for our further progressive development. According to Jim Collins, who coined the term, a BHAG is a mammoth, even mountainous, goal that stirs and stimulates a team, unifying and galvanising them into action. I would like to suggest that we have our BHAG be to make the godbody ideology a world class ideology by 2040. Of course, none of this means that I am blind to the fact that it is still up for debate what form our ideology should actually take, whether Black nationalist or Black thearchist.

Obviously, I stand in the camp of the Black thearchists: what I believe concerning the godbody is that our ideological positions must be based on the principles of the Black thearchy, principles such as the divinity of Black people; the devilishment of White people; the vampyrism of the Black bourgeoisie; the eroticism of the Black soul; the righteousness of the Five Percent Nation; the trick knowledge of White superiority; the revolutionism of Black illegality; the refinement of civilised teachings; the spookism of religious teachings; the syndicalism of the godbody parliaments; and the constant striving for a world of love, peace, and happiness. This is Black thearchism in the raw and the basis of our ideology must thereby be aligned with these principles; that is why as an ideology Black thearchism is superior to Black nationalism. It maintains godbody principles.

Though it could be argued that we godbodies castigate most of the Black masses by calling them the babies and most of the Black bourgeoisies by calling them the vampyres; if we come to appreciate that some within the Black community have sold their divinity to the devil, metaphorically speaking, to become Black leaders, and that most other Black people have been led astray by these Black leaders, then we can avoid making the same mistakes. Again, whether they have sold themselves to the devilishment of the White superiority discourse or surrendered to the power of the White supremacy perspective, the Black bourgeoisie have become vampyres to us, feasting on the blood of the lost Black masses. Thus demarcating clearly to Black people that we are not just another Black nationalist group is most important. We have various key doctrinal distinctions that separate us from the definitively Black nationalist, and our ideology must reflect that.

Consequently, the question of whether to fight for Black nationalism or Black thearchism is far more important – as to the direction of the godbody – than has been appreciated. While such a question has been treated as meaningless by some there are others who argue that national consciousness is in fact vital to our struggle. While I agree that national consciousness is vital to the *Black* struggle, to the godbody it only means going backwards. We have already evolved beyond national consciousness and community control. We must therefore seek for ourselves and our people a kind of God consciousness, consciousness of the divinity of self and kind.

Nationalism on its own is too bourgeois, too modern, too liberal, even if it is a Black nationalism. I am very passionate about this because bourgeois ideas and practices take from us the very essence of what makes us unique, and while certain bourgeois cultural niceties may be tolerable, and allowing certain bourgeois individuals to join our movement may be effective, if we surrender our ideology to the bourgeoisie, far from leading the people, we become the tail-end of the people. Our job and duty is to lead the people, not follow blindly the national struggle.

See, Black nationalism comes in two forms: revolutionary and reformist. The revolutionary element want Black Americans to select certain states to occupy and then to secede from the rest of America, forming a United

States of New Afrika, Ebonia, or whatever. Basically, a new country for Black Americans, led by Black Americans. They justify their right to have this separate nation with the exceptional circumstances under which Black Americans came to America and what they did in America after their kidnap. "Lincoln promised us forty acres," so they say. Well, if we added up all the descendants of slaves living in America and gave them each forty acres, then a land mass around about the size of Georgia and part of South Carolina would belong to this Black America. Therefore, they say they have the right to take a portion of the United States as their own. These Black nationalists are also usually quite militant, at least in rhetoric, and want an end to White supremacy.

At the other end of the spectrum: reformist Black nationalists are more for fighting to elect Black representatives in the US government, whether on a local or national level. The biggest victories to these individuals were the elections of Barack Obama as the first Black President, and of Kamala Harris as the first Indian Vice President. To these reformist nationalists change is possible within the United States and it is preferable to remain within the United States than to attempt to build a new country from scratch.

Both forms of Black nationalism are bourgeois and based on bourgeois standards. We in the Five Percent have a far more complex and effective political theory, but there are some who wish to take us backward to national consciousness. The Father, however, did not believe in the national struggle, hence, why he told us not to marry according to the government. The only nation he believed in was the Nation of Gods and Earths. The national-state is thereby rendered useless to us. It is the national-state that sends its police to arrest and murder us, it is the national-state that uses its judiciary to tarnish our record, it is the national-state that makes laws to favour those that are against us, and it is the national-state that created a system so complicated that the children of White people get a superior education to the children of the ghetto.

Black nationalism seeks to reinforce the national-state not abolish it, therefore it is of the utmost importance that we decide whether we will struggle with the Black nationalists to teach national consciousness or rise above the national struggle and fight with the Black thearchists to teach God consciousness. Following the masses and trusting in the spontaneous enlightenment of the masses rather than consciously bringing enlightenment to them will only degrade and dilute our movement. Black Lives Matter was powerful and important but we must guide the now nationally conscious Black people towards God consciousness.

To a degree it is a little opportunistic to say that the Black movement, in particular its manifestation as BLM, is better left to the spontaneity of the Black masses. The Black masses of the West are particularly indoctrinated into bourgeois nationalism from a young age. This indoctrination means that left to their own devices they will instinctively move towards nationalism, and reformist nationalism at that. Again, it is the devils and vampyres who have indoctrinated them into bourgeois nationalism; it is thereby the job of the godbodies to be more doctrinaire with regard to our teachings.

In this, while the Black vampyres of the 10 percent are predominantly bourgeoisies, and most of them reformist Black nationalists, it is our duty to educate, not only the Black masses of the 85 Percent, but even the Black vampyres of the 10 percent. That means educating them in the concepts, purpose, and BHAG of our movement. As they get deeper in these lessons they will come to learn the vision they are to strive for and reach with consistency in order to move closer towards further fulfilling our destiny. The more dogmatic and doctrinaire we become concerning our vision and objectives, the less likely we are of being corrupted over the years, and the better chance we have of converting the vampyres into Gods and Goddesses.

There is also another danger inherent in making the target of our BHAG refining a nationally conscious vision and not a God conscious one; we may lose our credibility as leaders in the Black struggle. We have a duty to civilise Black people, guiding and directing them towards achieving our goal. Yet if our ideology is merely Black nationalism and not Black thearchism, then they can look to the vampyres, who have led them thus far already, and they will have all that they need. Truly, the vampyres make far more effective advocates of national consciousness than us.

Yes, we are already Black thearchists, but I worry that this light subservience to nationalism may prove to be our downfall, making us undifferentiated from the other Black nationalist groupings. Vampyrism comes in three main forms, and we cannot risk allowing one of those forms to turn us all into vampyres. At the same time, nationalism is a preliminary step for the Black masses; first, is racial self-consciousness (actuated in Critical Race Theory); second, is national consciousness (actuated in Nationalist and Decolonial Theories); and finally, is God consciousness (which is actuated in our own Godbody Theory).

Consequently, many of us love to claim that our duty is to educate Black people, thus seeing ourselves like a vanguard for the Black struggle. Well, as Lenin said in his own time, the other contingents must first recognise us as the vanguard otherwise we lead nobody. Imagine walking up to a bourgeois vampyre, and many of them are high intellectuals, and saying that our duty is to educate them. They will no doubt ask themselves, "Have we bourgeoisies not been educating the masses these many decades? Who are these upstarts who claim to educate us? What makes them any more educated than us? Indeed, we promote the national struggle more so than they do, and we have a firmer grasp of intellectual concepts. Their own intelligence notwithstanding, we far exceed them in our understanding of Black theoretical concepts, Black national consciousness, and the history of the Black struggle. We are also far better trained and have far more connections within the establishment. We will allow them this conceit in saying they are educating us, but for all, we shall continue doing what we have been doing all along." So if we truly wish to exorcise the vampyrism of these Black bourgeoisies we must share with them a different message from the one they have been sharing these many decades.

All that said, we will now need to consider the objectives we will have to perform in order to accomplish this vision. First, there is what Jim Collins called, again: the Hedgehog Concept. To explain this he shared the story of the fox and the hedgehog: the fox is crafty, cunning, quick, and dangerous, much stronger and far more sophisticated than the lowly hedgehog. The hedgehog, on the other hand, is dowdy, ugly, and much slower and clumsier than the fox. Usually the hero of most European folk tales, the fox wins every time. However, whenever the fox, with his multiplicity of moves and tactics, jumps in front of the hedgehog to catch him, the hedgehog just performs one simple move and the fox is defeated every time. Curling up into a ball, with spikes pointing in every direction, the fox stands no chance and has to admit defeat.

In order to find our own hedgehog concept, we need to, first of all, understand for ourselves that as with any social movement/social enterprise we have an opportunity to build a business model around membership and franchising. This is important and it will be clear how important it is later on. Next, we will need to ask ourselves a very important question: what problems do we so effectively solve that would make anyone consider our social movement/social enterprise worth funding? When we look at the situation from this perspective and *honestly* appraise ourselves through this lens then it becomes very obvious that for most of our existence as a social movement – while we may have been masters of helping other people to gain a knowledge of themselves – we have not really taken the time to know our own selves as a social movement/social enterprise.

While, again, it could be said that our overall strength is that we have democratised divinity, what does that even mean to an ordinary person in the world? So then, how would *I* answer the funding question? I would say that the problem we solve is: we empower people of every race, particularly of the Black race, that seek their own empowerment. Understanding that, it should now become clear that we have the opportunity and responsibility to make sure we are paid for our service to the Black community, for our Allah Schools, and for two programmes I hope we can build in the future that I call the Allah College and the Allah Institute. The systems here expressed are fleshed out in greater detail in Chapter 6, which itself goes through the methodology by which we can organise and franchises our business model (ciphers, Squares, research facilities, parliaments, schools, colleges, and institutes) and provides a systematic blueprint that can be rolled out suggestion by suggestion, in different communities across America and the world.

All this provides a great beginning as it can add deep levels of clarity and focus, allowing us to appreciate where we are most helpful and vital. From this beginning we now move up and on to the formalising and systematising of a brand strategy by which the practicalities of how we enact our business model on a regular basis can be understood. There are consequently four aspects to brand strategy: brand definition, brand method, brand persona, and brand lifestyle. Our brand definition is found in our vision and what make up our vision. I would suggest that our brand method be that of the iconic brand (the examples being Red Cross, Red Crescent, Nike, and Apple). Having given it a lot of thought I would suggest that our brand personas be D'Angelo and Foxy Brown as both have studied 120 and both respected the godbody movement. Finally, our brand lifestyle will be discovered through the practicalities of our Hedgehog Concept.

The practicalities themselves, however, can be found for us, not in the 120 lessons, but in the Build Allah Square lessons, as explicated by Sunez Allah: (i) Eat, (ii) Train, (iii) Read, (iv) Write, and (v) Share. Nevertheless, three of these in particular will be of interest to us here: train, read, and write. Admittedly, growing up in Brooklyn, New York I only really knew the training aspect of the Square: the fighting ring in which "punks jumped up to get beat down". At the same time, back then if anyone presented some unfounded information, or broke any godbody rules, they may also end up in the Square getting "beat down."

But all this was done in love and for the purpose of training, so that if one of us was ever attacked they could defend themselves and their friends (a move that was especially helpful for the female godbodies, who themselves went into the Square with other female godbodies). The Square was thus effectively how we would train ourselves in various forms of mixed martial arts; and thereby gain strength, discipline, and confidence as we walked the streets of New York City. This was actually one of the main things I used to love about the godbody and is perhaps the best part of being God, that same confidence of knowing that if you were ever attacked you could fight back, and that even if you were winning in a fight and another God or Goddess saw you in the fight they would be obligated to jump in and help defend you in the fight.

Obviously, there can be detected in this an avenue towards our credibility, as our current use of violence is condemned by society with no proper understanding of its purpose or of its connection to martial arts training – which society currently recognises as itself a legitimate practice. Furthermore, can also be detected the analogy of an army nation; an analogy which is quite fitting as, like with any army, we ourselves are at war, our war is with the entire world system. Moreover, the band-of-brothers idea and reality also permeates our counter-culture. It is written in the Bible: "Hereby perceive we the love of God, because he laid down his life for us: and we ought to lay down our lives for the brethren" (1John 3: 16). Such an injunction may seem excessive and too difficult for most of the more squeamish members of modern Christianity, however, those in the military tradition live this principle every single day without complaint, resentment, or insubordination (at least for the most part).

Again, the analogy of an army for the godbody movement works well with the conception of our potential personal mission as presented earlier: to make the godbody ideology a world class ideology by 2040. And to be sure, we all know we could die at any time, therefore we must literally love our brothers and sisters in godbodyism to the point of being ready to die for them. Nevertheless, this is where the analogy ends, as in actually existing godbody ciphers and parliaments a captain's and a lieutenant's main duties are merely to guide the discussion and preside over the Build Allah Square, not to domineer over the soldiers nor any of the young Gods or Goddesses.

Remember also that the training element of the Square is not only for protection and confidence purposes, but also to keep godbody members from harbouring any bad or negative feelings towards their fellow brother or sister; this is because we need to be ready to die for these people should the worst go down. We *are* an Army Nation, and we usually exist within an oppressive nation that is at war with us. Notwithstanding, all godbody elders, older Gods and Goddesses, whatever their rank within the movement, should have a key position of leadership at our parliaments and ciphers based largely on their physical age.

Moreover, this training aspect of the Square actually and mainly works on three levels: (i) if somebody presents lessons or ideas that go against godbody lessons and ideas they may end up in the Square with six other Gods getting beat down for 90 seconds, (ii) if someone breaks any of the rules of the godbody they could also end up in the Square with six other Gods getting beat down for 90 seconds, and (iii) if a God has any kind of problem with another God for whatever reason: be it jealousy, humiliation, disrespect, fear, not picking up their phone when they called, or even looking at them funny, the two Gods would fight it out in the Square, one-on-one, in front of all the other Gods and Goddesses for 90 seconds, without needing to give the reason for wanting to go in the Square with that particular God. In each of these Square situations, no matter who wins the fight, who looks good in the fight, who looks weird or ridiculous in the fight, or who gets knocked out in the fight; when the fight is over all is not only forgiven it is also forgotten, and those same Gods are ready again to die for each other, and that is literally die. The same is also true for female godbodies going into the Square with other female godbodies.

But though with regard to this training aspect of the Build Allah Square we should be as dogmatic as with everything else, we must still always remember its real life consequences in illegalism, violence, and in sexual train-running, which thereby challenge the moral status quo. Still, that is only because we currently tend to judge by White standards. Technically, if we throw away White standards our illegalism, violence, and sexual train-running could actually be an example to the people. As far as train-running goes, we should not seek to initiate anyone into this practice while they are too young, but eventually they will still have to have sex someday. We can teach them the right way, with class and civilisation, even when running a train. This is the secret. Illegalism, if practiced as a form of social revolutionism, can be positive; violence, if practiced to defend oneself and/or loved ones, can be positive; and running a sexual train, if practiced as a form of free love with consent and responsibility, can be positive. Thereby, one can negotiate how one practices these godbody methods; without sacrificing the *realities* of the godbody lifestyle: which also includes these darker elements.

The main reason for the martial training aspect of this godbody lifestyle is to make sure that we all have genuine love for each other and not a fake, hypocritical, or delusional love for each other. Our lives are literally on the line in the street life so we have to literally be ready to die for each other. This means we have to be *willing* to die for each other, not harbouring resentment, animosity, or embarrassed feelings towards one another for whatever reason. While this darker aspect of the godbody lifestyle is real and visible, another element that was also quite real and quite visible was how well read most New York City thugs were. Those who were the biggest thugs in the street life were also highly intelligent. These were intellectual thugs who were autodidactic and deeply knowledgeable. Such a thirst for knowledge obviously had its origins in the godbody understanding that knowledge is infinite and that knowledge is the foundation, however, it also obviously had its roots in the read aspect of the Build Allah Square.

We, however, must now seek to develop this reading principle of the Square into a study and research principle for future generations. That means becoming masters of R&A. It also means developing facilities in our communities that rival those of the top colleges and universities. Not to say that we can rival the Harvards and the Princetons right now, but we have every reason to aim towards that destination. It is my heartfelt hope that we can see in ourselves the possibility of becoming not only intellectual thugs, but world class intellectuals. Period. Again, our research and analysis may not be limited to only reading books and articles but we must try to make it include reading books and articles as the more authoritative knowledge is usually found in books and in academic journals. Of course, this will also obviously mean joining academic associations so as to keep up with the current knowledge of issues related to our area of research, but it will all be helpful.

Conversely, having university level research facilities may seem like a daunting task, but we call ourselves scientists so we must behave as scientists. All scientists do research and back up their research with evidence, so we must try to have our own research facilities at least by 2050 so that we can do so too. In order to get there we will have to do something very few of us have really had the stomach to do before, but will have to learn how to do if we wish to move forward as a movement: request donations from larger

Black businesses and organisations. This sort of self-promotion will require the further building of our brand cache. As an example, Collins said quite provocatively, "Does Harvard truly deliver a better education and do better academic work than other universities? Perhaps, but the emotional pull of Harvard overcomes any doubt when it comes to raising funds. Despite having an endowment in excess of $20 billion, donations continue to flow" (Collins 2006: 25). Hereby, building research facilities in our ghettos may actually be a lot easier than we have so far thought, all we need to do is break it down into small simple steps that we can accomplish day-by-day.

Though this may all be fine and well, in our current form we have still failed to live up to the entirety of Sunez Allah's vision for the Square. There are currently too few godbody writings and too few godbody books. If we are to be truly faithful to the Square in its entirety we will need to write more and publish more. What I have done with mechanical analysis is provide us with a methodology on which to base our theories, to learn more about it you can read from my book *Demystifying God*, still, we must address new topics in society, the world, and in the sciences from this perspective. This way we expand beyond Knowledge 120 and move into Wisdom 240. Publishing books and articles means we lead the Black community towards progress, empowerment, and divinity through our ideology. Whether we choose to publish through an academic journal, through Draft 2 Digital, through KDP, or through a traditional publisher, the godbody movement must aim to have no non-authors by 2040, NONE. Obviously, if using Draft 2 Digital or KDP we should also be sure to go to Fiverr for our cover design, and to purchase David Gaughran's book *Let's Get Digital* so as to understand the full process of self-publishing. It is absolutely free and shows that getting a book published is not that difficult. Indeed, reading and research may be essential but we already do that more than enough, what we really need to do is write more and publish more.

As can be seen, these three central elements of the Build Allah Square play a major part in the application of our solution. At this point, it is all about discovering, based on this simple blueprint, what was called by Jim Collins "piercing clarity about how to produce the best long-term results [through attaining a] deep understanding of three intersecting circles: 1) what you are deeply passionate about, 2) what you can be the best in the world at, and 3) what best drives your economic engine." However, he also said, "Whereas in business, the key driver in the flywheel is the link between financial success and [an economic engine], I'd like to suggest that a key link in the social sectors is brand reputation – built upon tangible results and emotional share of heart – so that potential supporters believe not only in your mission, but in your capacity to deliver on that mission" (Collins 2006: 17, 25).

Having already discussed certain godbody general practices; and also presented these practices as solutions to common ghetto difficulties faced by the people; we can move on to the process of finalising our own Hedgehog Concept by consolidating all the information we have considered so far, plus using the three circles to achieve this end. It is thereby that I believe the best Hedgehog Concept for the godbody movement would be: we empower Black people intellectually, sexually, and martially, gaining greater brand equity per Build Allah Square initiated.

For those godbodies that still feel unworthy of funding now I should remind you every godbody is a supergenius when it comes to emotional intelligence. To face the trials of love, sex, stress, life-or-death consequences, heartbreak, pain, shame, the fall-out from shame, hyperaggression, hypervindictiveness, confusion, elation, style, survival, and still not only look cool while doing it, but be cool under the pressures of it takes a level of emotional gymnastics the average investment banker could never imagine. Herein, our Hedgehog Concept must remain our primary, central, and essential focus so that we do not forget who we are. Indeed, we may even have to learn to hyperfocus specifically on the fulfilment of this concept, as Collins further noted, "exercising the relentless discipline to say, 'No thank you' to opportunities that fail the hedgehog test" (Collins 2006: 17).

Moving on, Collins further presented to us another principle from his theoretical framework for social movement/social enterprise success: the flywheel principle. According to Collins, "In building a great institution, there is no single defining action, no grand program, no one killer innovation, no solitary lucky break, no miracle moment. Rather, our research showed that it feels like turning a giant, heavy flywheel. Pushing with great effort – days, weeks and months of work, with almost imperceptible progress – you finally get the flywheel to inch forward. But you don't stop. You keep pushing, and with persistent effort, you eventually get the flywheel to complete one entire turn. You don't stop. You keep pushing, in an intelligent and consistent direction, and the flywheel moves a bit faster. You keep pushing, and you get two turns … then four … then eight … the flywheel builds momentum … [Until] at some point – breakthrough!" (Collin 2006: 23).

For us in the godbody movement we fulfil this principle through the constant and consistent sharing of the message of What We Teach: (1) That Black people are the Original people of the planet earth. (2) That Black people are the fathers and mothers of civilization. (3) That the science of

Supreme Mathematics is the key to understanding man's relationship to the universe. (4) That Islam is a natural way of life, not a religion. (5) That education should be fashioned to enable us to be self-sufficient as a people. (6) That each one should teach one according to their knowledge. (7) That the Black man is God and his proper name is ALLAH. Arm, Leg, Leg, Arm, Head. (8) That our children are our link to the future and must be nurtured, respected, loved, protected, and educated. (9) That the unified Black family is the vital building block of the nation.

Each of these essential ideas are helpful and can provide talking points for all godbodies, anytime we try to teach those in the Black community. However, there are other elements and aspects to godbody theory that were not mentioned there, and that is fine, the solving of the problems we fight to solve through sharing the message of What We Teach will ultimately be how we turn the flywheel. Even subject matters like White supremacy, devilishment, vampyrism, Islamophobia, autophobia, homophobia, transphobia, misogynoirism, and genocide must only be spoken of within the context of one of these: the general ideas of What We Teach. It is thereby that we maintain focus, unity, order, and consistency as a movement. That said, they become mere trivialities and formalities if we do not enforce strict discipline with regard to our understanding of them.

The final objective that we as godbodies will need to develop is what Jim Collins called: the 20 Mile March method. To explain the 20 Mile March methodology Collins pointed out several indicators to determine whether a company was on its own 20 Mile March. Three of these will be of particular interest to our own social movement/social enterprise. Firstly, "A good 20 Mile March has *self-imposed constraints*. This creates an upper bound for how far you'll march when facing robust opportunity and exceptionally good conditions. These constraints should also produce discomfort in the face of pressures and fears that you should be going faster and doing more" (Collins 2011: 42). Having myself given this subject a lot of thought I have come to appreciate that for us this upper bound should be based on cautiousness over who we allow to franchise our movement and also receive our deeper lessons. This means not growing or accepting new members or new franchisees at a rate that is too fast for us to handle. There must therefore be a process, a long process, of preparation, probation, and qualification/disqualification, before one can be an authentic godbody member.

If a person or franchise is disqualified they will then need to begin the process all over again from the start to have a hope of future acceptance but we should not deny anyone the right to join or start a godbody franchise on the basis of race, class, gender, sexual orientation, bodily trans-formation, physical ability, or religious identity. Herein we hereby protect and demarcate our movement from the potential corruption that may be employed by the allowing of members from all these various social groups, each having their own social agenda they wish to advance. Through this method we will be able to maintain and promote a dogmatic stance on our vision and the objectives used to fulfil it, while still being able to influence, interact with, and associate with those outside of our movement.

We must therefore determine within ourselves that we will have as our upper limit a decision that regardless of threat, bribe, promise, popularity, or governmental pressure (of both the positive and the negative type) we will not allow any new godbody franchises or godbody members to be recognised until they have been through, first, a preparation period, then, a long probation period, during which time they will still be able to be disqualified and have to start the preparation process all over again: No questions asked. This will hopefully not mean that we become an elite within the ghetto, or that we overprice access to our franchise model. Historically, the ability to join the godbody and learn the teachings has always been free or at least easy, and I do not in any ways seek to change that. However, what I do seek to do is make access to membership and the lessons a little harder to attain.

While that may seem or sound counter to the wishes and method of Allah, as I said, this should merely be adopted: Firstly, to keep us from growing too fast for us to control during the following years. Secondly, to keep us from being seduced and corrupted by wealth and power when it joins and becomes a part of our movement. Thirdly, to keep us focused on what our teachings are and not distracted by side missions and other agendas, as important as they may be. Finally, to develop within ourselves and within those on the outside a level of exclusivity for our movement; that it is not just some simple non-profit begging for members to join but an exclusive club only few notables will be able to join.

Secondly, "A good 20 Mile March uses *performance markers* that delineate a lower bound of acceptable achievement. These create productive discomfort, much like hard physical training or rigorous mental development, and must be challenging (but not impossible) to achieve in difficult times" (Collins 2011: 40). Definitively, in employing the 20 Mile March method the godbody movement will have to choose a lower bound of performance that we must be sure – and also do our utmost – never to fall below. That means setting up systems of criticism, correction, and punishment to prevent the potential abuse of the freedom that can exist within any movement. Again, having given the subject a great deal of thought I have come to appreciate that this lower limit should be based on our attendance at godbody meetings, which we call parliaments; so by organising workers' parliaments for all godbody workers in any majority Black business, corporation, or organisation that function like TCs; consumers' parliaments in any godbody neighbourhood that function like DCs; and students' parliaments in any university where there is a godbodies presence that function like SUs we allow for the instituting of godbody values IRL.

Just for the record, having ghetto parliaments does not make us a parliamentarian organisation. Remember, most of us tend to be anti-state and far closer to syndicalism than parliamentarianism. Here our parliaments are like councils designed to discuss any issues facing the godbody as a movement. This concept of using parliaments as councils to discuss politics, economics, and social issues for the Black and ghetto communities I have affectionately called Black syndicalism. Yet in declaring that these godbody parliaments are thus syndicalist meeting grounds I have also effectively given us another way to identify our own social movement with the anarchic tradition. Now that does not mean that I believe we godbodies should automatically identify ourselves as Black anarchists either. As Bey said, "One does not, in short, *need* to call oneself a Black anarchist to be doing Black and anarchic work" (Bey 2020: 9).

Again, this form of 20 Mile Marching effectively "imposes order amidst disorder, consistency amidst swirling inconsistency. But it works only if you actually achieve your march year after year. If you set a 20 Mile March and then fail to achieve it – or worse, abandon fanatic discipline altogether – you may well get crushed by events" (Collins 2011: 43). It is herein that syndicalism, as an economic system, creates a far more suitable counter to the economic systems of modernity, socialism and capitalism, than anything postmodernism currently offers. As Brown also said concerning syndicalism, "The Syndicalist method is not organisation from the top down but from the bottom upward" (Brown 1990: 12). Indeed, the fact is that if the godbody hope to reach the 85 Percent who are not in leadership positions then syndicalism may be the only way to get to them.

It is quite plausible that the godbody would now ask why we should seek to infiltrate the workplace of majority Black or godbody owned businesses to set up workers' parliaments when trade unions already exist. The fact, however, is that a large number of unions are controlled by bureaucracy and struggle to get things moving. What I am suggesting to the godbody is that they instead lead and guide the Black workers to control themselves, to be their own saviours and their own managers. All this is in the tradition of anarcho-syndicalism, which "supports workers in a capitalist society gaining control over parts of the economy, and emphasizes solidarity, direct participation, and the self-management of workers. Additionally, anarcho-syndicalism has the aim of abolishing the wage system, seeing it as inextricable from wage slavery" (Bey 2020: 13). Indeed, workers would make far more effective managers of the work they have mastered doing than any newcomer who has only mastered the art of time management.

Furthermore, how this Black syndicalism would work would be similar to how anarcho-syndicalism worked when it did work. "The basis of the Syndicate [would be] the mass meeting of workers assembled at their place of work, factory, garage, ship, loco shed or mine. The meeting [would elect] its factory committee and delegates." "In the case of smaller individual shops, as these are usually found in groups (as grocers, chemists, butchers, bakers, etc.) about cross-roads or minor thoroughfares, workers from each shop would meet to elect their group committee" (Brown 1990: 35, 52). These committees could effectively co-ordinate with the neighbourhood consumers' parliaments in their locale to see what the consumers would like them to contribute to the social product based on their own qualifications and employment and what they are able potentially to contribute to the social product based on their capacity.

But these workplace workers' parliaments will not only be co-ordinating with the neighbourhood consumers' parliaments of their locale, they will also be co-ordinating with other bodies of workers' parliaments: "The factory Syndicate [should be] federated to all other such committees in the locality – textile, shop assistants, dockers, busmen and so on. In the other direction the factory, let us say engineering factory, [would be] affiliated to the District Federation [or Parliament] of Engineers. In turn the District Federation [would be] affiliated to the National Federation of Engineers" (Brown 1990: 35), and we could probably squeeze a regional parliament between the district and the national for all workers', consumers', and students' parliaments too.

Finally, "A good 20 Mile March must be *achieved with great consistency*. Good intentions do not count" (Collins 2011: 42). So long as we attend these parliaments with consistency within our godbody communities, we will create far greater co-ordination and structure than currently exists within the chaotic market and far greater efficiency and functionality than currently exists within the lethargic state. Ultimately, we godbodies should have in our arsenal three kinds of parliaments: the workers', the consumers', and the students' parliaments. Obviously we should not seek to do things like running trains at any of these parliaments, though such should be encouraged and respected within our own godbody communities. The eating and training aspects of the Square, however, can be practiced during a cipher. Still, the reading and writing aspects of the Square can primarily be practiced at our workers', consumers', and students' parliaments.

Even so, most ideas of the thearchy are not in some utopia, panacea, ideal, nirvana, or Shangri-La; they are an actually existing movement for those seeking to find Allah, teaching them traditions and a counter-culture that will ultimately help them to find Him within. Basically, giving them access and the ability to see their own divinity despite their astral, social, or global realities. However, this outlook also brings us into conflict and confrontation with the current standards and views of both Eurocentric civilisation and Americanised modernity. These views, based on what socialists have called bourgeois rights, are at present contrary to human nature and the reality of human imperfection. These bourgeois rights, in themselves, are the product of historical developments and not genuine justice or ethics in any essential sense: for the justice of Allah is found only in his universal laws and his divine love.

The Beginnings of a New Cosmology

The purpose of this chapter is to reflect on the constitution of a godbody cosmology and what connects it fundamentally to an Islamic Adamology. As we can see from all this, Islam is beyond what we can describe with human words, and that it takes a special tongue, one of divine origin, to speak the words of Islam. Yet there have been many to do just that. True, Adam was the first human *Nabi* (prophet), Muslim, and *Khalifah*, but in a technical sense every prophet was also a Muslim and a *Khalifah*. This is the area of *Nubuwwa* (prophethood), that state that is beyond what we in our time are able to reach. Indeed, the ancient prophets were guides and showed us how to find truth: for this cause we seek Allah, not in new prophets or in new prophecies but in the fulfilment of his truth. In fact, the truth of Allah is Allah himself. Allah is the Absolute Truth and the Absolute Reality. Beyond Allah there is nothingness, yet, at the same time, Allah reaches into nothingness and pulls out creation.

This also reveals a dialectic in the universe: the famous dialectic of being, non-being, and becoming, or said another way presence, absence, and arriving. Allah is *al-Mawjud* or the omnipresent: he dwells in presence and can only be present in all things. At the same time, the Quran says of him, "He is the First and the Last and the Manifest and the Hidden, and He is Knower of all things" (Quran 57: 3). Allah manifests himself in his creation, hence the term *tawhid*. The concept of *tawhid* – when it is appreciated that Allah and his creation are one, that Allah is manifested through his created things – thus proves to be closer to the reality of monism than monotheism. Herein, Allah and the universe are one, as it is also written in the Quran, "Now surely they are in doubt as to the meeting with their Lord. Lo! He surely encompasses all things" (Quran 41: 54).

So, what now does that mean? That Allah encompasses all things but inanimate mud? Or that Allah encompasses all things but subatomic waves? Or that Allah encompasses all things but plastic bags? Or even that Allah encompasses all things but evil people? Indeed, Allah encompasses all people, including you yourself – making both selfishness and selflessness equally fallacious, as Allah can manifest himself in all people and all things. Again, if Allah encompasses all things then he is in fact omnipresent (*mawjud*) and the *tawhid* is in fact a theocentric-monism; Allah is thereby seen and heard *everywhere*.

It is written again, "And there is not a thing but with Us are the treasure of it" (Quran 15: 21). That said, there are many treasures in heaven and on earth, but we shall now be focusing on the treasury of imagination. Ibn al-Arabi spoke of three forms of imagination: non-delimited imagination, objective imagination, and subjective imagination. Non-delimited imagination is also called the astral world, while objective imagination is the physical world, and subjective imagination is the imaginal world. Each of these worlds are encompassed in the *tawhid* even as Allah is Lord of all worlds. Moreover, each of these universes are parts of the body of Allah while the face of Allah could be called *al-Dhatullah*.

Again, as Allah is the Real or the True, his thoughts are a reality unto themselves. But some of what Allah imagines he then brings to life. It is written, "Our word for a thing, when We intend it, is only that We say to it Be; and it is" (Quran 16: 40). Allah adds being to his intentions by taking of his own Being, even as he is the Supreme Being. Ibn al-Arabi said, "God made imagination a light through which the assumption of forms by all things – whatever it might be, as we said – may be perceived. Its light penetrates into sheer nonexistence and gives it the form of an existence" (Ibn al-Arabi 1972; quoted from Chittick 1989: 122). Allah, who is Existence/Being injects being into his intention by saying to it "Be!"

And again, Allah is *Mawjud* (Existent). Allah is also *al-Haqq* (the Real or the True), even as it is written, "And We created not the heavens and the earth and what is between them but with truth [*haqq*]" (Quran 15: 85). What we can see from this is that Allah took of himself as *al-Haqq* and created the physical universe. As noted, the universe is effectively the body of Allah. The universe itself is, however, in a state between existence and nonexistence called becoming. Even deeper still, between being and becoming there is another *barzakh*, what ibn al-Arabi called the Supreme Barzakh. It stands between the Real and the coming to be. It is the realm of non-delimited imagination that many scientists call the astral plane and that the ancient people used to call the heavens.

Basically, in the beginning was Allah, the *Haqq*. The *Haqq* had a thought: non-delimited imagination. As it was his thought it was close to his reality, though it did not exist in existence as the only existent thing was Allah. Then Allah said to some of his thoughts, "Be!" and they came to be, thus they became his creation. However, none of those thoughts came to be immediately. In fact, their coming to be was and is a process. Nothing comes to be fully developed. Everything evolves till it becomes what it was supposed to be. Thus the realm of Being is the Real, the realm of non-delimited imagination is the Astral Realm, the realm of constant evolution is the physical realm, and the realm of personal thought is the subjective realm. Each *barzakh* containing its own rules and its own laws.

See, I acknowledge the Asiatic Black man as divine by nature, but one cannot deny the forces that exist in the universe and operate in a manner that shows order beyond what is encased in this flesh. Those forces operate under the laws of electromagnetism (the other laws being gravitational force, bonding force, radioactive force, and strong force are merely different amplitudes of this one force, at least that is the way I see it). Electromagnetic is not a mystery nor is it a spook in the sky that cannot be seen with the physical eye; it is a force that we can prove exists scientifically. It is my view that this force is Allah as this force is the creator of all life, the physical and the astral entities. Not that I am saying electromagnetic should be worshiped – though no self-respecting godbody would worship any outside force whatsoever, someone reading this book may think it is what I am suggesting – however, electromagnetic is energy and matter in their purest form. Furthermore, the atoms in our universe are all bought together by electromagnetism; but electromagnetism can be seen to affect more than atoms if viewed in a new light. This is how Allah "is seen and is heard everywhere" as just mentioned.

To explain what I mean I will use the example of bonding force; all atoms are apparently very subtle entities: they repel at close distances, become connected at intermediate distances, and attract at long distances. Bonding forces are usually considered separately so as to acknowledge the scientist who discovered them, but are really just the same electromagnetism being based on electric fields and magnetic fields. Gravity too, if looked at this way, can be perceived as nothing more than an extension of electromagnetism as the earth has an electric and a magnetic field. While this theory is still a little adolescent and my ability to show and prove may be a little weak I can say that attraction in its rawest state is a force, and while Newton agreed that there are two kinds of attractive forces, inherent and impressed, he still divided them into two different categories, magnetic and gravitational. The truth, however, is that perhaps what we have been seeing as gravity is really just electromagnetism and Newton's theory was useful for its time but now we can accept the magnetic pull of planets, moons, stars, and galaxies. Nevertheless, I must say this is all just theory.

If my theory is correct then the truth becomes self-evident: electromagnetic has been shown to be related to radioactivity and strong force, it is obviously also connected to chemical bonding, and gravity itself may even be a typology of its force. Yet electromagnetic is an energy wave. While we may concede that neither energy nor matter are primary entities but both are manifestations of something deeper and unknown to science, I will not here argue that this something is Allah, I will simply return to Einstein's $E = MC^2$; C is a constant and to Einstein that constant was the speed of light. One thing we know for sure from this is that light itself is a form of electromagnetism at a certain wavelength. This is proven. Based on these hard facts, light, electricity, atoms, molecules, fluids, chemicals, minerals, metals, planets, stars, moons, sun, and all life-forms – including humanity – all came from electromagnetism. If we are looking to make Allah real we should look no further. And these are only manifestations on the physical plane not to mention the astral plane.

The astral plane is definitely produced by electro-magnetism, in fact, it is most likely the realm of the so-called spirit seen by the apostles and prophets, and seen by most people in their dream state. It is a creation of the mind generated by the electricity in our brainwaves. This electricity produces an electric field, and where there is an electric field there is also a magnetic field as its counter. The mind has an electromagnetic field which transports the being or soul to the astral plane, like the hand of Allah grabbing the prophet Ezekiel by the locks of his head (Ezekiel 8: 3). If astral beings exist then their body would be of pure electromagnetic energy even as it says in the Holy Quran: "And We indeed created you, then We fashioned you, then We said to the angels: Make submission to Adam. So they submitted, except Iblis; he was not of those who submitted. He said: What hindered thee that thou didst not submit when I commanded thee? He said: I am better then he; Thou hast created me of fire, while him Thou didst create of dust" (Quran 7: 11, 12). Again, the word translated as fire is *nar* which – given our modern knowledge – would better translate as electrical energy. Thus Iblis (Lucifer), the angels, and the *jinni* (daemons) are here shown to be beings of massless light, which appear as electromagnetism.

In the third place, electromagnetism also stimulates our senses to bring about a reaction from our body. The skin and flesh feel, the tongue tastes, the nose smells, the ears hear, the eyes see, the brain perceives, and the erotogenous zones orgasm. The seven senses of touch, taste, smell, sound, sight, supersensoriality, and sensuality are all products of electromagnetism. I cannot claim expertise on the deeper recesses of each of these subjects; however, I can say that it is through electromagnetism that the senses make real the world we live in, even as a photon (electromagnetic wave) can carry an image or images; and a radiowave (also a kind of electromagnetic wave) can carry sound.

Everything we know and ever can know comes to us only via electromagnetism. So while electromagnetism carries the keys to omnivision, omniscience, omnipotence, omnipresence, sensuality, metamorphosis, and creation and destruction (while itself being uncreatable and indestructible), I also appreciate that the Asiatic Black man is divine in his own way, and through mastery of sensuality and mastery of supersensoriality – that is, mastery of clairvoyance, clairaudience, *clairalience, clairgustance,* clairsentience, and *panopathy* (which itself is being an elemental empath, thus having a deep understanding of *lithopathy, hydropathy, pyropathy, pneumopathy,* and *cryopathy*; being a environmental empath, thus having a deep understanding of *climateopathy, germopathy, agripathy,* zoopathy, and telepathy; and being a universal empath, thus having a deep understanding of *biopathy, electropathy, technopathy, cosmopathy,* and *chronopathy*) – he also has the ability to attain to divinity. (Though most people call the sixth sense extrasensory perception I prefer to call it supersensory perception due to its clearer perception). But again, all these ideas border on the pseudoscientific so I will simply move on for now.

There have been many prophets throughout history all of them with methods for their own time on how to manifest divine attributes. In our time we have the scholars who use the divine Shari'a in more conclusive ways so as to accomplish this end. The scholars also have the words of all the prophets and the lessons of all former scholars throughout history. Through these they have been able to narrow down the *Shari'at u'llah* into twelve Universal Laws of Existence:

1. *The law of interaction (whose corollary is the pleasure principle),*
2. *The law of intersubjectivity (whose corollary is the vibratory law),*

3. *The law of self-organisation (whose corollary is the identity law),*
4. *The law of opposition (whose corollary is the feedback law),*
5. *The law of repetition (whose corollary is the inertia law),*
6. *The law of self-similarity (whose corollary is the correspondence law),*
7. *The law of conservation (whose corollary is the reciprocity law),*
8. *The law of evolution (whose corollary is the power law),*
9. *The law of devolution (whose corollary is the entropy law),*
10. *The law of self-destruction (whose corollary is the phase-transition law),*
11. *The law of interconnectivity (whose corollary is the synchronicity law), and*
12. *The law of interrelation (whose corollary is the eternalist law).*

Again, these *Shari'at u'llah* (laws of God) cannot be broken, therefore they are not only the laws of the Supreme Barzakh but are also the laws of the entire creation.

Yet within the reality of these *Shari'at u'llah* can also come miraculous abilities (*karamat*). Within cultural Islam there are four main types: *panopathy* (*al-rahmat ul-mutlaq*), which comes by mastering the second Universal Law of Existence; acting through resolve (*al-fi'l bi'l-himma*), which is another way of saying telekinesis and comes by mastering the third Universal Law of Existence; manifesting into engendered existence (*takwin*), which comes by mastering the eleventh Universal Law of Existence; and supersensory perception (*ma'nawi idrak*), which comes by mastering all twelve Universal Laws of Existence. While these are all achievable through falling into states, they become permanent attributes only through entering into a station. Effectively, when one finds oneself performing miraculous signs it generally means they have entered upon a state and are in that moment expressions of Allah's power but states themselves are only achievable through release of libidinal energy. The more libidinal energy you feel towards someone (or the One) the more likely you are to enter upon a state.

Though it is true that prophets no longer exist in the world as an established office, we in the godbody do have dervishes possessing one or more of these gifts: *rahmat ul-mutlaq* (*panopathy*), *himma* (telekinesis), *takwin* (manifesting), and *ma'nawi idrak* (supersensory perception). These gifts exist to those who enter upon a state, and can be reached through them taking the sexual energy they achieve in orgasm or multiple orgasms and focusing it on mastering the practices of the station they are currently in. They should not try to seek to skip stations. Though while it could technically be said that our fate is already written, the relativity of our agency allows for some leeway, and just as for the male, achieving a state or reaching a station is interdependent on their relation with women, so to a woman, achieving a state or reaching a station is interdependent on their relation with men. Ultimately, however, whether one has reached a station or is simply in a state one is still able to do what all the prophets were able to do even in our time.

The main distinction in our time is that we have received unveilings rather than prophecies. One who has not reached a station can still fall into a state, while states become less likely as one rises up the stations. Chittick (1989: 278) said on this subject, "the 'state' (*hal*) or present spiritual situation of the individual is by definition transitory, while a 'station' (*maqam*) may have the same attributes as a state except that it is a fixed quality of the soul. States are 'bestowals' while stations are 'earnings.'" Conversely, it is impossible to reach a station outwardly that you have not also reached inwardly.

What we have learned in the final summation is that in Islam there are several theories of humanity that are addressed: (i) humanity has the same origin as all other things in nature, (ii) the Original people were made from the same elements as are found in the earth, (iii) the Original people were Black people, (iv) the forces of nature can be mastered by humanity, (v) what gives life meaning is libido, (vi) what differentiates humanity from the animals is knowledge, libidinal sublimation, and the *Khalifah*, (vii) the different races and languages all exist as a sign to teach us how to live, (viii) Original people are the *Shaitan* of Iblis and Iblis is the *Shaitan* of the Original people, (ix) racialisation was an Islamic practice but racial stratification was not, (x) racial awareness and the vying with different races was seen as virtuous, (xi) the universal laws are based on the shari'a of Allah, (xii) there are signs one can perform through mastering different aspects of the shari'a of Allah, (xiii) one who performs signs by faith has entered into a state, and (xiv) one who performs signs by knowledge has entered into a station. Based on all this we can see that Islam has a far more viable Adamological framework from which to view different social and racial groupings. Thereby the godbody Adamology, based on Islamic sociology, has a philosophy of man far superior to what humanism could ever be.

Conclusion

If we were to look deeper into the concept of ideology itself, we would be able to find, according to Heywood, that it is really nothing more than: "a more or less coherent set of ideas that provides the basis for organized political action, whether this is intended to preserve, modify or overthrow the existing system of power" (Heywood 2017: 10). Recognising, moreover, that though James Cone did say that ideology was just the objectification of a viewpoint: we also know that ideology can actually be subjective, indeed, intersubjective through empathic interrelations. Therefore, as I envision it: just as neo-Labourism was basically a communitarian liberalist ideology; even so, neo-Islamism should be seen as a utilitarian thearchist ideology, though in fact it is actually far more than that due to the definition of neo-Islamism being anarcho-Islamism.

I have therefore also tried throughout this book to demonstrate the closeness of the godbody tradition to that of the anarchist tradition; and though I am also able to say with Bey, "I care little … about bringing people into the institutional fold of anarchism", I do care about anarchic themes that demonstrate themselves through godbody interpretations and illustrations. We godbodies, as believers in and practitioners of righteousness, and as refusing to be corrupted by pressures from the United States government to submit to their authority; already have striking similarities to anarchism that we definitely need to appreciate.

Hereby, due to the current illegalism of some of our members, and our own aggressive hatred of the police, most of us are already anti-state seeing the state as a means of oppression against the people that corrupts nations. While some of us may be willing to work with the government to fight for social change, for the most part the government is deemed just as corrupted as the state it directs. Ultimately, we godbodies seek the overthrow of the state and its replacement with ghetto parliaments and ciphers. This is the second area where godbodyism agrees with anarchism: we have a syndicalist structure. Our parliaments operate similar to labour councils and would be very effective as labour councils if put into practice as such. A third area where godbodyism is similar to anarchism is with the use of social revolutionism, predominantly illegalism. Though most anarchists are ideologically social revolutionaries we godbodies have thus far had no ideological training. But our righteousness is an even higher righteousness than that of the state, whose laws we do not recognise, therefore there is some serious significance to our illegalism. Finally, our prohibition of marriage according to the government means that we also advocate for free love, and some even go so far as practicing plural love. In these ways we have much in common with anarchism, so it is my hope that through introducing these truths to us godbody I may help us to achieve the goal of becoming a world class Black ideology in the near future.

It is in the hopes of promoting this godbody outlook to both Christians and Muslims that I have attempted to answer some extraordinary issues that might arise due to its ideas. Though, obviously better suited to Muslims, this philosophy works well even with any Christians willing to adopt it. Understandably, a common judgment or accusation levelled against any new or challenging ideas is the stigma of cult, or belonging to a cult; as noted earlier, this book should be read as an Islamist book, or perhaps, more accurately, as a neo-Islamist theological treatise. The heart and soul of the book itself is to effectively allow my Black people to go to their mosque, church, or other religious gathering, and identify the divinity in themselves and their own Black brothers and sisters. Thereby to allow all we Black people to reach a far better place of emancipation, decolonisation, and empowerment than we have ever reached before.

Notwithstanding, there are still currently, and have been for the longest time, numerous doomsday predictions of future nuclear holocaust, fascist dystopia, or post-apocalyptic tragedy. These ideas, to some degree or another, all seem to coincide with the Hobbsian state-of-nature theory of human internal depravity and corruptibility. Here the best version of society is what we have now, i.e., the modern status quo. Yet the current move is one geared towards assisting this modernism in its own self-destruction. It pushes forward the march against the evils of modernity (colonialism, World War I, the October Revolution, the rise of Fascism, World War II, the Holocaust, and the Atomic bomb). What I have hopefully shown to the reader is that within the current social system lies a disturbing contradiction that must be addressed in all these issues of modernity and thereby overcome: the current ideology of White supremacy.

Obviously, there are other areas of this theory that still need tweaking, however, as a form of Black ideology this could take godbodyism very far. Ultimately, the Black thearchy developed throughout is a kind of countercultural, hypersexual, theocentric, postsecular, supra-religious, neo-libertine, trans-utilitarian, quasi-Freudian, socio-Newtonian, ultra-Darwinian, eroto-masochist, proto-seductionist, light-exhibitionist, semi-essentialist, anti-racist, beta-militarist, pan-eternalist, bio-monist, inter-subjectivist, and Négro-theist perspective and lifestyle. Though this variation in itself may not be the common version of godbodyism it is the Shahidian version I myself have chosen to adopt and encourage for those willing to join me and the rest of the Black thearchists in our struggle to overcome all the ills of the modern status quo.

Series Postscript

Though this series is and will be very controversial throughout, especially for one who is a self-proclaimed Black theologian. Nevertheless, considering that the Black thearchy I have herein sought to promote to the world is neither a corrupt authoritarian, nor a chaotic utopian, system, but in fact an already existing ghetto movement, our motive is not the ultimate overthrow of existing bourgeois society. All we seek is merely the defending of our actually existing culture, traditions, and doctrinal viewpoints, even as they currently stand, and not the allowing of any modernist standards or opinions to corrupt them or contaminate any of our existing doctrinal interpretations; regardless of the level of persecution we receive for carrying them.

In modern society the main and central differentiation between revolutionary deviance and criminal malevolence is a matter of internal perspective: just like "one man's terrorist is another man's freedom fighter." Distinction is also perceptible through a person's level of internal consciousness. Or to better clarify, the central disparity between a criminal and a freedom fighter *is* their level of consciousness. Yet using such a reductionist simplification one could draw the further conclusion that all that really distinguishes a freedom fighter from the divine is, in this case, their level of *habba* (libido). Here, through altering perspectives we can hopefully attain to a raising of *habba*, and thereby of divinity in the street life.

Ultimately, through strengthening the social forces of ghetto culture we can effectively begin the process of abolishing White privilege, and overthrowing this whole corrupt system of White supremacy. Herein, the godbody movement provides a wealth of guidance, and access to many lessons that may prove quite complex. For this cause, if you currently wish to learn more about our movement (I get paid nothing for this endorsement), feel free to write to the address below:

> The Allah School in Mecca
> 2122 7th Avenue
> New York, NY 10027
> USA

Also be sure to let them know that it was a book in this series that inspired you to join. Once they have been informed as to your true intentions they should be willing to give you everything you need to be an enlightened part of this movement.

Lastly, I have really enjoyed writing this book; and as a part of my *Black Divinity Series* it has been a key facet and aspect of my life's work as a theologian and biblical scholar. For this cause, I currently make this final request: that if you have gained or learned anything you feel to be of value please remember to leave a review on the platform from which you purchased this book. Small things like that help authors like me gain wider readership and validation for our efforts. They also give us the opportunity to hear some of stories of those we have touched with our work. Thank you for your support, much love and peace.

Attention African American Theologians!!!

Learn Now a Black Cosmology Designed Purely for the Ghetto

The Universal Order of Things is the fifth Instalment in Shahidi Islam's *Black Divinity Series*. Is there an ideal cosmology for Black people? How about for Black ghetto people? Shahidi Islam provides a type of the cosmology he learned growing up in Brooklyn, New York. To learn more about it shop now.

The Universal Order of Things

Bibliography

Abraham, N (1994); "Notes on the Phantom a Complement to Freud's Metapsychology." In N. T. Rand (Ed), *The Shell and the Kernel*; University of Chicago Press.

Abraham, N (1994); "The Phantom of Hamlet or The Sixth Act preceded by The Intermission of 'Truth'." In N. T. Rand (Ed), *The Shell and the Kernel*; University of Chicago Press.

Abraham, N & Torok, M (1994); "Mourning or Melancholia: Introjection Versus Incorporation." In N. T. Rand (Ed), *The Shell and the Kernel*; University of Chicago Press.

Abron, J. M (2005); "'Serving the People': The Survival Programs of The Black Panther Party." In C. E. Jones (Ed), *The Black Panther Party [Reconsidered]*; Black Classic Press.

Adler, A (1964); *The Individual Psychology of Alfred Adler: A Systematic Presentation in Selections From His Writings*; Harper & Row, Publishing, Inc.

Adogame, A (2011); "Introduction." In A. Adogame (Ed), *Who is Afraid of the Holy Ghost: Pentecostalism and Globalization in Africa and Beyond*; Africa World Press.

Afrika, L (2013); Dr Llaila Afrika We Are Different; http://m.youtube.com/watch?v=r6aaP6Ynoj4, accessed in May 2014.

Albert, M (2004); *Parecon: Life After Capitalism*; Verso

Alexander, M (2011); *The New Jim Crow: Mass Incarceration in the Age of Colorblindness*; The New Press.

Aptheker, H (1996); "Maroons Within the Present Limits of the United States." In R. Price (Ed), *Maroon Societies: Rebel Slave Communities in the Americas*; The John Hopkins University Press.

Asante, M. K (2003); "The Afrocentric Idea." In A. Mazama (Ed), *The Afrocentric Paradigm*; Africa World Press, Inc.

Asante, M. K (2013); "Afrocentricity Imagination and Action." In V. Lal (Ed), *Afrocentricity Imagination and Action*; Multiversity & Citizens International.

Ashby, M (2003); *Sacred Sexuality: Ancient Egyptian Tantric Yoga The Neterian Guide to Love, Sexuality, Marriage, Relationships and the Secrets of Sexual Energy Cultivation, Sublimation, and Spiritual Enlightenment*; Sema Institute of Yoga.

Avineri, S (1968); *The Social & Political Thoughts of Karl Marx*;
Cambridge University Press.

Baudrillard, J (2012); *Simulacra and Simulation*; The University Press.

Bauman, Z (2016); *Liquid Modernity*; Polity Press.

Bauman, Z (2003); *Identity Conversations with Benedetto Vecchi*; Polity Press.

De Beauvoir, S (2009); *The Second Sex*; Vintage Classics.

Ben-Jochannan, Y (2002); *The Need for a Black Bible*; Black Classic Press.

Bey, M (2020); *Anarcho-Blackness: Notes Toward a Black Anarchism*; AK Press.

Blackburn, R (1988); *The Overthrow of Colonial Slavery 1776-1848*; Verso Books.

Bor, M, and Bor, J (2024); *Come Together: Trades Councils 1920-50*; The Book Guild Ltd.

Brandchaft, B, Doctors, S, and Sorter, D (2010); *Toward an Emancipatory Psychoanalysis: Brandchaft's Intersubjective Vision*; Routledge.

Brown, F, Driver, S and Briggs, C (2014); *The Brown-Driver-Briggs Hebrew and English Lexicon*; Hendrickson Publishers.

Buber, M (2008); *I and Thou*; Simon & Schuster.

Callinicos, A (2003); *An Anti-Capitalist Manifesto*; Blackwells Publishing Ltd.

Chittick, W (1989); *The Sufi Path of Knowledge*; State University of New York Press.

Chittick, W. C (2013); *Sufism: A Beginner's Guide*; Oneworld Publication.

Chomsky, N (1999); *Profit Over People: Neoliberalism and Global Order*; Seven Stories Press.

Chomsky, N (2003); *Understanding Power: The Indispensable Chomsky*; Vintage Books.

Chomsky, N, Foucault, M (2006); *The Chomsky-Foucault Debate On Human Nature*; The New Press.

Chomsky, N, Achcar, G (2007); *Perilous Power: The Middle East and US Foreign Policy Dialogues on Terror, Democracy, War and Justice*; Penguin Books.

Chiu, C-y, Leung, A, K-y, Hong, Y-y (2011); "Cultural Processes: An Overiew." In A. K-Y. Leung, C-Y Chiu & Y-Y Hong (Eds), *Cultural Processes: A Social Psychological Perspective*; Cambridge University Press.

Churton, T (2015); *Gnostic Mysteries of Sex: Sophia the Wild One and Erotic Christianity*; Inner Traditions.

Collins, J (2006); *Good to Great and the Social Sectors: A Monograph to Accompany Good to Great*; Random House Business.

Collins, J (2020); *Good to Great*; [ONLINE] Available at: https://www.audible.co.uk/webplayer?asin=147359202X&contentDeliveryType=SinglePartBook&ref_=a_min erva_cloudplayer_147359202X&overrideLph=false&init ialCPLaunch=true. [Accessed 07/12/2023].

Collins, J & Porras, J. I (2005); *Built to Last: Successful Habits of Visionary Companies*; Random House Business Books.

Cone, J. H (2012); "Theology's great sin: silence in the face of white supremacy." In *The Cambridge Companion to Black Theology*, eds. Dwight N. Hopkins and Edward P. Antonio; Cambridge University Press.

Cone, J. H (2018); *Black Theology and Black Power: Fiftieth Anniversary Edition*; Orbis Books.

Cone, J. H (2020); *A Black Theology of Liberation: 50th Anniversary Edition*; Orbis Books.

Daulatzai, S (2012); *Black Star, Crescent Moon: The Muslim International and Black Freedom Beyond America*; University of Minnesota Press.

Davis, D (1984); *Slavery and Human Progress*; Oxford University Press.

Degnbol-Martinussen, J, Engberg-Pedersen, P (2005) *Aid: Understanding International Development Cooperation.* London: Zed Book Ltd.

Diop, A (1991); *Civilization or Barbarism*; Lawrence Hill Books.

Douglas, K. B (1999); *Sexuality and the Black Church: A Womanist Perspective*; Orbis Books.

Durkheim, E (2014) *The Rules of Sociological Method: And Selected Texts on Sociology and its Method.* New York: Free Press.

Durkheim, E, Mauss, M (2009); *Primitive Classification*; Taylor & Francis.

Ehrman, B. D (2003); *Lost Scriptures: Books that Did Not Make It into the New Testament*; Oxford University Press, Inc.

Elias, N (2014) *The Civilizing Process*. Oxford: Blackwell Publishing.

Engberg-Pedersen, P, Gibbon, P, Raikes, P, Udsholt, L (1996) *Limits of Adjustment in Africa: The Effects of Economic Liberalization, 1986-94*. Suffolk: James Curry Ltd., Heinemann, Reed Publishing.

Engels, F (1947); *Anti-Dühring Herr Eugen Dühring's Revolution in Science*; Progress Publishers.

Foner, P (2002); *The Black Panther Speaks*; Da Capo Press.

Fanon, F (1964); *Toward the African Revolution*; Grove Press.

Fanon, F (1965) *A Dying Colonialism*; Grove Press.

Fanon, F (1969); *The Wretched of the Earth*; Penguin Books.

Fanon, F (2008) *Black Skin, White Masks*; Pluto Press.

Feuerstein, G (1998); *Tantra: The Path of Ecstasy*; Shambhala Publications, Inc.

Foucault, M (1998) *The History of Sexuality Vol. 1: The Will to Knowledge*; Penguin Books.

Foxe, J (2001); *Foxe's Book of Martyrs*; Bridge-Logos Publishing.

Franco, J. L (1996); "Maroons and Slave Rebellions in the Spanish Territories." In R. Price (Ed), *Maroon Societies: Rebel Slave Communities in the Americas*; The John Hopkins University Press.

Freeden, M (2013); "The Morphological Analysis of Ideology." In M. Freeden, L. T. Sargent, and M. Stears (Eds), *The Oxford Handbook of Political Ideologies*; Oxford University Press.

Gahlin, L (2007); *Egypt: Gods, Myths and Religion*; Anness Publishing Ltd.

Gentles-Peart, K (2016); *Romance with Voluptuousness: Caribbean Women and Thick Bodies in the US*; University of Nebraska Press.

Gilroy, P (1999); *The Black Atlantic: Modernity and Double Consciousness*; Verso.

Gladwell, M (2002); *The Tipping Point: How Little Things Can Make a Big Difference New Edition*; Abacus.

Gladwell, M (2009); *Outliers: the Story of Success*; Penguin Books.

Gleick, J (1998); *Chaos: The Amazing Science of the Unpredictable*; Vintage Books.

Goldman, E (1911); *Marriage and Love*; Mother Earth Publishing Association.

Gordon, L (2012); "Requim on a Life Well Lived: In Memory of Fanon." In N. Gibson (Ed), *Living Fanon: Global Perspectives*; Palgrave Macmillan.

Grady-Willis, W. A (2005); "The Black Panther Party: State Repression and Political Prisoners." In C. E. Jones (Ed), *The Black Panther Party [Reconsidered]*; Black Classic Press.

Gramsci, A (1971); *Antonio Gramsci: Selections from the Prison Notebooks*; Lawrence &Wishart Ltd.

Graves-Brown, C (2010); *Dancing for Hathor: Women in Ancient Egypt*; Continuum Books.

Greene, R (2004); *The Art of Seduction*; Profile Books.

Grinker, R, Lubkemann, S, Steiner, C (2010); *Perspectives on Africa: A Reader in Culture, History, and Representation Second Edition*; Blackwell Publishing Ltd.

Hardt, M, Negri, A (2000) *Empire*; Harvard University Press.

Harman, C (1999); *Economics of the Madhouse*; Bookmarks Publications Ltd.

Harrison, L (2002); "On Cultural Nationalism." In P. Foner (Ed), *The Black Panther Speaks*; Da Capo Press.

Harvey, D (2006); *Limits to Capital*; Verso Book.

Hawass, Z (2006); *The Royal Tombs of Egypt*; Thames & Hudson Ltd.

Hayes, F. W, III, Francis, K. A, III (2005); "'All Power to the People': The Political Thought of Huey P. Newton and The Black Panther Party." In C. E. Jones (Ed), *The Black Panther Party [Reconsidered]*; Black Classic Press.

Herring, G (2006); *Christianity: From the Early Church to the Enlightenment*; Continuum International Publishing Group.

Heywood, A (2017); *Political Ideologies: An Introduction*; Palgrave.

Hill, N (2004); *Think and Grow Rich Revised and Expanded by Dr Arthur R. Pell*; Vermillion London.

Hudson, M (2021) *Super Imperialism: The Economic Strategy of American Empire Third Edition*. Dresden: ISLET-Verlag.

Huntington, S. P. (1996); *The Clash of Civilizations and the Remaking of World Order*; Simon & Schuster, Inc.

Ibn Katheer Dimashqi, H (2006); *Book of the End: Great Trials and Tribulations*; Maktaba Dar-us-Salam.

Imseis, A (2010); "Speaking Truth to Power: On Edward Said and the Palestinian Freedom Struggle." In A. Iskandar and H. Rustom (Eds), *Edward Said: A Legacy of Emancipation and Representation*; University of California Press.

Intelexual Media (2023); *A Short History of Masturbation*; [ONLINE] Available at:
https://www.youtube.com/watch?v=0aoY6Ihjips.
[Accessed 29/11/2023].

Jackson, S. A (2009); *Islam and the Problem of Black Suffering*; Oxford University Press.

Jacobs, M (1992); *Key Figures in Counselling and Psychotherapy:*
Sigmund Freud; Sage Publications Ltd.
Johnson, O. A (2005); "Explaining the Demise of The Black Panther Party: The Role o Internal Factions." In C. E. Jones (Ed), *The Black Panther Party [Reconsidered]*; Black Classic Press.
Jones, W. R (1998); *Is God a White Racist? A Preamble to Black Theology*; Beacon Press.
Josephus, F (2013); *The Works of Josephus: New Updated Edition*; Hendrickson Publishers.
Karenga, M (1989); *Introduction to Black Studies*; University of Sankore Press.
Katz, A (2008); *The Holocaust: Where Was God? An Inquiry into the Biblical Roots of Tragedy*; Burning Bush Press.
Keen, D (2012); *Useful Enemies: When Waging Wars is More Important than Winning Them*; Yale University Press.
King, M. L, Jr (1986); *A Testament of Hope*; HarperCollins Publishers.
King, M. L, Jr (1992); *I Have A Dream; Writings and Speeches That Changed the World*; HarperCollins Publishing.
Koester, C (2014); *Revelation*; Yale University Press.
Koestler, A (1976); *The Thirteenth Tribe*; Random House, Inc.
Kolawole, M. E. M (1997); *Womanism and African Consciousness*; African World Press.
Kropotkin, P (2002); *Anarchism*; Dover Publications Inc.
Kropotkin, P (2006); *Mutual Aid: A Factor of Evolution*; Dover Publications Inc.
Kumar, D (2012); *Islamophobia and the Politics of Empire*; Haymarket Books.
Knight, M. M. (2011); *Why I Am a Five Percenter*; Penguin Group.

Lear, J (1998); *Love and Its Place in Nature: A Philosophical Interpretation of Freudian Psychoanalysis*; Yale University Press.

Lenin, V (1968); *V. I. Lenin Selected Works*; Lawrence and Wishart Ltd.

Lenin, V (2010); *Imperialism: The Highest Stage of Capitalism*; Penguin Books.

Lenin, V (2014); *State and Revolution*; Haymarket Books. Square Press, Inc.

Lenin, V (2020); *What Is to Be Done? Burning Questions of Our Movement*; Science Marxiste.

lil' bill (2023); *How Black Elites LIE to Us*; [ONLINE] Available at: https://www.youtube.com/watch?v=Uu-X_E8cwaA. [Accessed 29/11/2023].

Littlewood, R (2006); *Pathology and Identity: The Work of Mother Earth in Trinidad*; Cambridge University Press.

Lizokin-Eyzenberg, E & Shir, P (2021); *Hebrew Insights From Revelation*. Israel: Jewish Studies for Christians.

Luxemburg, R (2004); *The Rosa Luxemburg Reader*; The Monthly Review Press.

Lyotard, J (1986); *The Postmodern Condition: A Report on Knowledge*; Manchester University Press.

MacCulloch, D (2010); *A History of Christianity*; Penguin Random House.

Mackenzie-Grieve, A (1968); *The Last Years of the English Slave Trade Liverpool 1750-1807*; Frank Cass & co. Ltd.

Malcioln, J (1996); *The African Origins of Modern Judaism*; Africa World.

Marx, K (1986); *Capital Volume I*; Lawrence &Wishart Ltd.

Marx, K (1958); *Selected Works vol 3*; Foreign Languages Publishing House.

Maxwell, M (1998); *Revelation: Doubleday Bible Commentary*; Bantam Doubleday Dell Publication Group, Inc.

M'Bantu, A, Muller, G (2013); *The Ancient Black Hebrews and Arabs*; Pomegranate Publishing.

McHugo, J (2019); *A Concise History of Sunnis & Shi'is*. London: Saqi Books.

McRobbie, A (2008); *Pornographic Permutations*; Routledge.

Meiu, G. P (2011); "'Mombasa morans': embodiment, sexuality and Samburu men in Kenya." In S. Tamale (Ed), *African Sexualities: A Reader*, Pambazuka Press.

Meyer, M, W (1992); *The Gospel of Thomas: The Hidden Saying of Jesus*; Harper.

Moltmann, J (1993); *Theology of Hope: On the Ground and Implications of a Christian Eschatology*. Minnesota: Fortress Press.

Muhammad, E (1965); *Message to the Blackman of America*; Muhammad's Temple of Islam No. 2.

Newton, H (2002); *The Huey P. Newton Reader*; Seven Stories Press.

Nkrumah, K (2006); *Class Struggle in Africa*; Panaf Books.

Nkrumah, K (2009); *Consciencism Philosophy and Ideology for De-Colonization*; Monthly Review Press.

Nkrumah, K (2022); *Neo-Colonialism: The Last Stage of Imperialism*; African People's Conference.

Nye, J S, Jr (2004); *Soft Power: The Means to Success in World Politics*; Public Affairs Books.

Nzegwu, N (2011); "'Osunality' (or African eroticism)." In S. Tamale (Ed), *African Sexualities: A Reader*, Pambazuka Press.

Patterson, O (1996); "Slavery and Slave Revolts: A Sociohistorical Analysis of the First Maroon War, 1665-1740." In R. Price (Ed), *Maroon Societies: Rebel Slave Communities in the Americas*; The John Hopkins University Press.

Philo (2016); *The Works of Philo: Complete and Unabridged New Updated Edition*; Hendrickson Publishers Marketing, LLC.

Raja, M (2020); *Decolonizing Literary Theory: Some Tentative Thoughts | Zahiriyya and Bataniyya Philosophy*; [ONLINE] Available   at: https://www.youtube.com/watch?v=Ez7UZUCM8wo. [Accessed 06/12/2023]

Rand, N. T (1994); "New Perspectives in Metapsychology: Cryptic Mourning and Secret Love." In N. T. Rand (Ed), *The Shell and the Kernel*; University of Chicago Press.

Rand, N. T (1994); "Secrets and Posterity: The Theory of the Transgenerational Phantom." In N. T. Rand (Ed), *The Shell and the Kernel*; University of Chicago Press.

Reddie, A. G (2008); *Working Against the Grain: Re-imaging Black Theology in the 21st Century*; Routledge.

Roberts, A (2011); *Evolution The Human Story*; Dorling Kindersley Limited.

Roberts, J. D (2012); "Dignity and destiny: black reflections on eschatology." In *The Cambridge Companion to Black Theology*, eds. Dwight N. Hopkins and Edward P. Antonio. Cambridge: Cambridge University Press.

Rowland, C (1985); *Christian Origins: An Account of the Setting and Character of the most Important Messianic Sect of Judaism*; SPCK.

Said, E (2003) *Orientalism*. London: Penguin Books.

Saraswati, S (2012); *Kundalini Tantra*; Yoga Publications Trust.

Sardar, Z, Abrams, I (2012); *Introducing Chaos: A Graphic Guide*; Icon Book Ltd.

Schimek, J-G (2011); *Memory, Myth, and Seduction: Unconscious Fantasy and the Interpretive Process*; Routledge.

Seale, B (2002); "The Ten-Point Platform and Program of the Black Panther Party." In P. Foner (Ed), *The Black Panther Speaks*; Da Capo Press.

Seleem, R (2004); *The Egyptian Book of Life*; Watkins Publishing London.

Seligman, C. G (1966); *Races of Africa*; Oxford University Press.

Shari'ati, A (1979); *On the Sociology of Islam: Lectures by Ali Shari'ati*; Mizan Press.

Shari'ati, A (1980); *Marxism and Other Western Fallacies*; Mizan Press.

Shari'ati, A (1981); *Man & Islam*; Islamic Publications International. [ONLINE] Available at: https://www.amazon.co.uk. [Accessed 01/03/2023].

Shari'ati, A (2002); *Where Shall We Begin? Enlightened Thinkers and the Revolutionary Society*; Citizens International.

Shari'ati, A (2003); *Religion vs. Religion*; ABC International Group.

Shari'ati, A (2006); *Civilization and Modernization: What's the Difference*; Citizens International.

Shari'ati, A (2011); *The Islamic Renaissance Series: Capitalism Wakes Up!*; [Kindle App Edition]; ABJAD Book Designers and Builders. [ONLINE] Available at: https://www.amazon.co.uk. [Accessed 19/11/2022].

Sheller, M (2012); *Citizenship From Below: Erotic Agency and Caribbean Freedom*; Duke University Press.

Singh, N. P (2005); "The Black Panthers and the 'Undeveloped Country' of the Left." In C. E. Jones (Ed), *The Black Panther Party [Reconsidered]*; Black Classic Press.

Skousen, M (2017); *The Big Three in Economics: Adam Smith, Karl Marx, and John Maynard Keynes*; Routledge.

Smif-N-Wessun (1995); "Home Sweet Home." In *Dah Shinin'* [CD]. New York: Wreck Records, Nervous, Inc.

Smif-N-Wessun (1995); "PNC." In *Dah Shinin'* [CD]. New York: Wreck Records, Nervous, Inc.

Snoop Doggy Dogg (1994); *Doggystyle*; Death Row Records.

St. Augustine (1958); *City of God*; Bantam Doubleday Dell Publishing Group, Inc.

Stourton, E (2005); *In the Footsteps of Saint Paul*; Hodder Headlin Ltd.

Strong, J (1990); *The New Strong's Exhaustive Concordance of the Bible*; Thomas Nelson Publishers.

Strachey, J (1936); *The Theory and Practice of Socialism*; Victor Gúllancz Ltd.

The Holy Bible: King James Version (2002); Michigan: Zondervan.

The Holy Qur'an: Maulana Muhammad Ali Translation (2002); Ohio: Ahmadiyya Anjuman Isha'at Islam Lahore Inc.

Torok, M (1994); "The Illness of Mourning and the Fantasy of the Exquisite Corpse." In N. T. Rand (Ed), *The Shell and the Kernel*; University of Chicago Press.

Turman, E. M (2018); "Heaven and Hell in African American Theology." In *The Oxford Handbook of African American Theology*, eds. Katie G. Cannon and Anthony B. Pinn; Oxford University Press.

Turner, L (2011); "Fanon and the Biopolitics of Torture: Contextualizing Psychological Practices as Tools of War." In N. Gibson (Ed), *Living Fanon: Global Perspectives*; Palgrave Macmillan.

Tyldesley, J (2011); *The Penguin Book of Myths & Legends of Ancient Egypt*; Penguin Books.

Umoja, A. O (2005); "Set Our Warriors Free: The Legacy of The Black Panther Party and Political Prisoners." In C. E. Jones (Ed), *The Black Panther Party [Reconsidered]*; Black Classic Press.

Van Loon, H (1960); *The Story of Mankind*; Washington Square Press, Inc.

Vanee, L (2023); *End the Genocide* [ONLINE] Available at: https://www.facebook.com/reel/1584869658715687. [Accessed 17/12/2023].

Wacquant, L (2016) "Bourdieu, Foucault, and the Penal State in the Neoliberal Era." In D. Zamora & M. C. Behrent (Eds), *Foucault and Neoliberalism*. Cambridge: Polity Press.

Watterson, B (2013); *Women in Ancient Egypt*; Amberley Publishing.

Williams, D. S (1993); *Sisters in the Wilderness: The Challenge of Womanist God-Talk*; Orbis Books.

Williams, D. S (2011); "Black Theology and Womanist Theology." In D. N. Hopkins & E. P. Antonio (Eds), *The Cambridge Companion to Black Theology*; Cambridge University Press.

Williams, J (1928); *Hebrewisms of West Africa From the Nile to the Niger with the Jews*; Africa Tree Press.

X, M (1968); *The Autobiography of Malcolm X*; Penguin Books.

X, M (2004); *Why I am Not an American*; Citizens International.

www.ingramcontent.com/pod-product-compliance
Lightning Source LLC
Chambersburg PA
CBHW071326140726
47996CB00005B/1836